To remain for such length of time as might, according to the circumstances of each individual case, be considered necessary as a term of probation, and for instruction in the means of obtaining an honest livelihood. The object of the Home was twofold. First to replace young women who had already lost their characters and lapsed into guilt, in a situation of hope. Secondly, to save other young women who were in danger of falling into the like condition, and give them an opportunity of flying from crime when they and it stood face to face.

The projectors of this establishment, in undertaking it, were sustained by nothing but the high object of making some unhappy women a blessing to themselves and others instead of a curse, and raising up among the solitudes of a new world some virtuous homes, much needed there, from the sorrow and ruin of the old. They had no romantic visions or extravagant expectations. They were prepared for many failures and disappointments, and to consider their enterprise rewarded, if they in time succeeded with one third or one half of the cases they received.

Charles Dickens
Home for Homeless Women – *Household Words*
23 April 1853

D0248755

Introduction

In 1908 a small number of probation officers met in a house in Croydon to plan the formation of the National Association of Probation Officers, later to become Napo. The previous year, in August 1907, the Probation Service came into being and it has now existed for 100 years. Ironically it reaches its centenary at a time when its future as a national service is uncertain. Whatever happens over the next period the word 'Probation' is in danger of being lost.

This book celebrates the work and achievements of the Probation Service over its first century. It restates its values through the words of retired members, through the main events in its and Napo's history, through images in film and television and through the comments of many individuals who have appreciated the contribution of the service over the last 50 years.

Retired staff, representing all grades, were interviewed over an eighteen month period in 2005/6. The individuals, who all belonged to a union at some time, came forward in response to requests in Napo News or were contacted through the Edridge Fund. Their careers and recollections span six decades from 1940 to 2002. Many talk of the days when female probation officers were not allowed to supervise men, when hats had to be worn by women staff in court, when all officers were involved in adoption work, and when innovation was encouraged and nurtured. Their comments all reflect a shared passion for the job and despite different approaches to the work a belief in their ability to bring about change.

Many talked of having large caseloads, doing home visits, 'walking the streets', recognising that their work involved an element of risk, working long hours and pioneering probation involvement in prisons.

Others record with fondness the introduction of community service, placing extreme importance on working in local neighbourhoods. Some were involved in innovative projects with the Black community, with Travellers, with women, with the mentally ill and with the homeless, or were involved in opening hostels in their earliest days. Most were involved in the service before the creation of ancillary posts. Some undertook training at University or College, others were direct entrants to the service and a few completed a Home Office course at Rainer House in London. All shared a delight at working in a team which many likened to being in an extended family.

The work of the Service attracted the attention of the makers of films and television drama, particularly in the 1950s and 1960s. Many of those programmes are featured in this publication. With the aid of the British Film Institute and Mike Nellis, from Glasgow University we present an

overview of this with stills from many of the productions. The highlight was probably the Associated Television production of The Probation Officer, which ran for three years from 1959 and starred, amongst others, Honor Blackman.

The history of the service is outlined through highlighting the main landmarks, important legislation and activities and developments within Napo.

Finally, Napo asked a number of eminent individuals, all with knowledge and understanding of the Service, to write a paragraph giving their thoughts on the Probation Service's contribution to the community over time. Their views are also reproduced.

We would like to thank those who shared their experiences with us and reminded us of positive days in the Service. In 2012 it will be the 100th anniversary of Napo. That event could well result in a sequel.

Harry Fletcher
Assistant General Secretary

Vicky Boroughs
Napo Vice-Chair (2003 - 06)

The evolution of Probation

The origins of probation dates back to the early years of the 19th century. Family court work had been a statutory part of the probation task since 1937. The notion of an association for staff emanates from discussions between probation officers at the turn of the last century.

The histories of Napo and the Probation Service have been intrinsically interwoven over the last 100 years.

The following are some significant events that have shaped the service and Napo's development.

3. **The Responsibility of a Probation Officer to his Colleagues**

(a) In his work a Probation Officer should remember that he is charged to carry out his duty very largely on his own responsibility and in his own way; he should therefore respect the individual judgment used by his colleagues in their approach to their work. The methods of one officer may be very different from those of another officer, but both may be equally and successfully applicable to differing situations.

Since then he has moved to a new home and is on good terms with his neighbours. Investigation showed that his previous offences were committed when he lived in a bad environment and there had been improvement when he moved. No further treatment is possible.

Highlights from Napo ephemera show how times have changed

Further enquiries would then be made into those aspects of your personal fitness for the work of a probation officer which cannot be assessed at an interview by a Selection Committee.   These include a medical examination, and X-ray of the chest if a report on a recent one is not available and, on occasion, a psychiatric examination to go into certain aspects of temperament that are known to be relevant to success or

/failure

R.S.V.P.

NATIONAL ASSOCIATION OF PROBATION OFFICERS,
29, GT. JAMES STREET, BEDFORD ROW, W.C.1.

MORNING DRESS.

"Hooliganism"

The existence of disorderly and ruffianly conduct among the juvenile population of London, especially in the streets, is traced by competent judges to a few clearly defined causes, all of which co-operate in the result.

WEDNESDAY
September 7th

10 am "Problems of John Citizen" – Mrs. A. Hawkins

2.45 p.m.

VOTE OF CONGRATULATION TO THE EARL OF FEVERSHAM on the occasion of his marriage to the Honourable Anne Wood.

1820

Warwickshire Magistrates pioneered a radical new sentence of one-days jail for young offenders on condition that they returned to the care of their parents or master 'to be more carefully watched and supervised in the future'.

1841

The Recorder of Birmingham extended the process of supervision to voluntary helpers or guardians who were asked to take immediate charge of young offenders released from the court.

1876

the first Police Court Missionary was appointed to Southwark and Lambeth Courts in London, 'for the purpose of dealing with individual drunkards, with a view to their restoration and reclamation'.

1879

The Summary Jurisdiction Act was passed which allowed Police Court Missionaries to help and advise persons discharged on their recognisance.

1896

The Police Court Mission opened its first shelter for boys in trouble in Camberwell.

1905

The first probation officers were appointed to Birmingham Children's Courts. The two individuals appointed were police constables who performed their duties in plain clothes.

A meeting of probation officers, Croydon, 1908

CHAPTER 25.

An Act to permit the conditional Release of First Offenders in certain cases.

A.D. 1887.

[8th August 1887.]

WHEREAS it is expedient to make provision for cases where the reformation of persons convicted of first offences may, by reason of the offender's youth or the trivial nature of the offence, be brought about without imprisonment:

Be it therefore enacted by the Queen's most Excellent Majesty, by and with the advice and consent of the Lords Spiritual and Temporal, and Commons, in this present Parliament assembled, and by the authority of the same, as follows:

1.—(1.) In any case in which a person is convicted of larceny or false pretences, or any other offence punishable with not more than two years imprisonment before any court, and no previous conviction is proved against him, if it appears to the court before whom he is so convicted that, regard being had to the youth, character, and antecedents of the offender, to the trivial nature of the offence, and to any extenuating circumstances under which the offence was committed, it is expedient that the offender be released on probation of good conduct, the court may, instead of sentencing him at once to any punishment, direct that he be released on his entering into a recognizance, with or without sureties, and during such period as the court may direct, to appear and receive judgment when called upon, and in the meantime to keep the peace and be of good behaviour.

Power to court to release upon probation of good conduct instead of sentencing to punishment.

(2.) The court may, if it thinks fit, direct that the offender shall pay the costs of the prosecution, or some portion of the same, within such period and by such instalments as may be directed by the court.

Inaugural meeting of Napo, Croydon, 1912

1907

124 male and 19 female missionaries to police courts were in post. Their remit had expanded to cover those in trouble for any cause. The Home Office recommended the creation of 'a society comprising and managed by the probation officers themselves'.

1907

The Probation Offenders Act was introduced. It's purpose was 'to enable the courts of justice to appoint probation officers, to pay them salaries or fees, so that certain offenders, whom the court did not think fit to imprison... might be placed on probation under supervision'. The duty of the officers was 'to advise, assist and befriend'.

1908

The Children's Act set up a separate Juvenile Court. The Home Secretary also allowed 'women of education' to work as probation officers in the London Juvenile Court.

1908

The first meeting of ten probation officers was hosted by Sydney Edridge, Clerk to the Justices, in a house in Croydon. It was called to discuss the formation of a staff association.

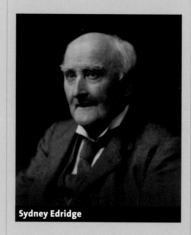

Sydney Edridge

CHAPTER 17.

An Act to permit the Release on Probation of
Offenders in certain cases, and for other matters
incidental thereto.   [21st August 1907.]

A.D. 1907.

BE it enacted by the King's most Excellent Majesty, by
and with the advice and consent of the Lords
Spiritual and Temporal, and Commons, in this present
Parliament assembled, and by the authority of the same,
as follows :

1.—(1) Where any person is charged before a court
of summary jurisdiction with an offence punishable by
such court, and the court thinks that the charge is proved,
but is of opinion that, having regard to the character,
antecedents, age, health, or mental condition of the
person charged, or to the trivial nature of the offence,
or to the extenuating circumstances under which the
offence was committed, it is inexpedient to inflict any
punishment or any other than a nominal punishment, or
that it is expedient to release the offender on probation,
the court may, without proceeding to conviction, make
an order either—

*Power of
courts to
permit
conditional
release of
offenders.*

    (i) dismissing the information or charge ; or

    (ii) discharging the offender conditionally on his
        entering into a recognizance, with or without
        sureties, to be of good behaviour and to appear
        for conviction and sentence when called on at
        any time during such period, not exceeding
        three years, as may be specified in the order.

1912

The National Association of Probation Officers held its first formal meeting at Croydon Town Hall. Sydney Edridge was the initiator and he became the first Chair. A unanimous resolution was passed 'that in the opinion of this meeting of probation officers, the formation of a National Association of such officers is in the best interest of their duties and is desirable and necessary'. The annual subscription was two shillings and six pence. The first AGM was held at Caxton Hall, London, moving in subsequent years to Anderton's Hotel, Fleet Street

1913

The first issue of the newsletter was published under the title 'The National Association of Probation Officers'. It was priced at one penny. The first Napo branch was opened in Huddersfield, Yorkshire.

1922

A report on the training, appointment, and payment of probation officers recognised the equal value of missionary (Family Court) work alongside work with those who commit offences.

First minutes book, 1912

Caxton Hall, site of the first Napo AGM

A boy 'before' and 'after' arriving on industrial training ship 'Clio', Menai Straits, North Wales. Front cover of Napo Newsletter, 1913.

Inaugural Meeting held at the Town Hall Croydon, May 22nd 1912.

Present, His Worship The Mayor, Mr Alderman Trumble (Chairman) Mr S G. Edridge. Clerk to the Croydon Borough Justices and Probation Officers for London and District Police Courts

1. Mr S.G. Edridge gave an address on probation Officers work. Pointing out the necessity for the formation of an association of Probation Officers

2. The following resolution were passed:

1.. (A) That in the opinion of this meeting of Probation officers the formation of a national association of such Officers is in the best interest of their duties, and desirable and necessary

(B) That a small committee be now formed to consider the necessary steps to be taken for the formation of such a Society

2. That in the opinion of this meeting of Probation Officers it desirable to present a memorial to the Home Office asking that an enquiry should be held as to the working of the Probation Act more especially respecting its operation with regard to =1 Reformatory and Industrial Schools, Training and Homes —

2. that the preparation of the memorial to be then

Detail from first minutes book, 1912

Anderton Hotel, Fleet Street
(AGM venue in the 1920s)

Glasgow probation office, 1926

Gertrude Tuckwell

1926

The Criminal Justice Act established a comprehensive probation service throughout England and Wales. The Home Secretary was given the power to prescribe salaries, probation committees were established and the use of probation was extended to the higher courts. Napo launched a campaign for a National Pension Scheme.

1927

Gertrude Tuckwell, the vice president of Napo raised a hospitality fund to enable Napo members to attend the annual conference and organised accommodation in private houses in London.

1929

The Probation Journal was launched under the patronage of the Earl of Feversham. He remained president of Napo until his death in 1963.

Regional conference, 1927

NATIONAL ASSOCIATION
of PROBATION OFFICERS

Nineteenth
Annual Conference

HELD AT

LIVINGSTONE HALL,
(Opposite St. James' Park Underground Station)
Broadway, Westminster,
S.W. 1.
MAY 20th & 21st, 1931.

President ..	The Rt. Hon. THE EARL OF FEVERSHAM, J.P.
Vice-Presidents ..	Miss GERTRUDE M. TUCKWELL, C.H., J.P.
	S. G. EDRIDGE, O.B.E.
	W. E. WILSON, J.P.
Chairman	W. CLARKE HALL.
Hon. Secretary	.. G. H. WARREN.
Hon. Treasurer	W. G. WORTHINGTON.
Hon. Auditor	.. J. TENNANT.
Secretary	.. H. E. NORMAN.

OFFICES :
29, Great James Street, Bedford Row, London, W.C. 1.

Telephone :
Holborn 4410.

Bankers :
Westminster (Parr's) Bloomsbury Branch.

Summer school Cheshunt College, Cambridge, 1934

1930

Napo's first head office was opened at 29 Great James Street, London, WC1. The Earl of Feversham raised funds to cover the rent and the salaries of two secretarial staff.

1933

The Children and Young Persons Act was implemented. It introduced the concept having regard to welfare, which had been steadily seeping through into the magistrates courts. It also made home surroundings reports necessary in all but the most trivial of cases.

ERECTED BY THE
NATIONAL ASSOCIATION OF PROBATION OFFICERS
AND FRIENDS
TO THE MEMORY OF
SYDNEY GEORGE EDRIDGE O.B.E.
WHO DIED 8th. MARCH 1934.
FOUNDER OF THE ASSOCIATION
CHAIRMAN 1912 TO 1928.

MAYOR OF CROYDON 1897-1898.
CLERK TO THE CROYDON BOROUGH MAGISTRATES
1899 TO 1925.

1934

Sydney Edridge died. A memorial was unveiled in Croydon Town Hall. The Edridge Fund was founded for 'serving and retired probation officers and their dependants in need'.

1937

The Summary Procedure (Domestic Proceedings) Act was passed, establishing that the task of matrimonial conciliation was part of a probation officer's statutory duties. Previously it had been limited to the 'Kindred Social Work of the Courts'.

Napo conference, Southport, 1957

1939

Probation was scheduled as a reserved occupation and the service was kept intact for the duration of the war.

1941

Responsibility for probation passed formally from the Police Court Mission to the Home Office. Napo elected a Chair from its membership for the first time. Napo also adopted a democratic constitution. Napo's head office in Whitehall was hit during night-time air raids.

1942

The first Principal Probation Officer Conference was held during the middle of the Second World War.

1945

Napo revised its constitution and for the first time achieved financial independence with a membership of 791. The Home Office also accepted Napo as the sole negotiating body for all probation officers.

Rainer House students, 1951

1948

The Criminal Justice Act introduced a new structure for the service extending responsibilities to aftercare. The duty of officers was endorsed as 'advise, assist and befriend'. It gave the Home Office the power to finance hostels and probation was integrated into the local government superannuation scheme.

1954

The Probation Christian Fellowship held its first meeting. Membership was open to all probation staff and others who worked with offenders and their families.

1956

Napo launched a major case for a salaries review. It was rejected by the Home Office. Napo referred it to an industrial court and won a higher than cost of living award.

1962

The Morrison Report was published supporting Napo's case for professionalisation. A probation officers' was 'a professional caseworker, employing in a specialised field, skills held in common with other social workers'. The committee recommended a bold increase in salaries.

A national pay pause meant that it was not implemented until 1964, when much of its impact was reduced.

1962

Napo's 50th anniversary was celebrated with a reception at St James's Palace attended by Princess Margaret and a gathering at Croydon addressed by the Archbishop of Canterbury.

1966

Prison Welfare Officers and social workers in detention centres became eligible to join Napo.

1967

The Probation and After-Care Service was established introducing the parole system. Women were allowed to supervise adult males for the first time. Previously female officers were only allowed to supervise women and girls and boys up to the age of 12.

1968

The Home Office introduced the post of 'ancillary worker' in a small number of areas as an experiment to relieve the caseloads of probation officers.

NATIONAL ASSOCIATION
OF PROBATION OFFICERS

NAPO

**PROCEEDINGS
of the
FIFTY-FIFTH
ANNUAL
CONFERENCE**

SCARBOROUGH
29th and 30th April
1967

Speakers
H. N. Grindrod
Megan Browne
Gordon Jones
Mark Winston
Dr. H. M. Holden
Lord Hamilton of Dalzell

4s 0d

60th AGM Llandudno, Jill Tibbits, Napo Chair 1969-72 (left) and Mr T Bales

1969

Probation in Scotland became part of the new social work service. It resulted in the loss of 200 Napo members.

1970

After a long debate Napo voted at a special AGM by 1160 to 499 not to join a unified social work association and thereby to continue as a separate organisation.

1972

The Government announced that the probation and after-care service would continue to be independent and not integrated with social services. Napo had campaigned against the merger.

1972

Community Service was introduced as a sentence of the court in six pilot areas. By 1979, it was available across England and Wales and extended the role of ancillary staff.

1973

The Napo Members Action Group was launched aiming to 'transform a professional association into a trade union'.

1974

The Butterworth Report concluded that the Home Office had underestimated the needs of the service. Napo demanded an agreed workload measure.

1974

The first ever conference for student probation officers was organised by Napo at Friends House, London. Over 200 attended the event from 36 courses.

1974

The first meeting of Gay and Lesbian Probation Officers and social workers was held at Conway Hall, London. 70 people were in attendance. Seven years later LAGIP was launched with the principal aim of offering support to members.

1976

NAPSAC (Napo Sporting Activities Club) was formed after the May AGM. It was supported by Napo president Lord Hunt. Its aim was to encourage social walking and climbing. The first event was the scaling of Snowdonia.

1978

Napo suspended its London Branch because of its presence on the Grunwick Photo Processing picket line. The suspension was rescinded by the 1978 AGM.

1980

The Kent Control Unit was opened and individuals were required to attend for six days a week for six months under the powers of the Criminal Courts Act 1973, which provided for attendance at a day centre as a condition of probation.

1982

Napo voted to expel any member who joined the breakaway organisation – the National Association of Senior Probation Officers. Subsequently a handful were expelled.

1983

Napo called its first ever one-days strike in protest at the reduction in probation trainee salaries. The act was described by Lord Donaldson as 'a monstrous, small but very ugly event'. Around 1,500 staff attended a Central London rally, addressed by amongst others, MPs Tony Benn and Clive Soley.

1984

The Association of Black Probation Officers was formally launched in February in London. Its aim was to support Black staff and to promote a Black view on professional issues.

Snowdonia Expedition

23-24 October 1976

Your climbing colleagues are currently training to reach the peak of condition but, when you summit up, the rock on which the expedition's success stands is financial support.

Sponsorship forms have been distributed by your local Edridge Representative.

It is abseilutely vital that everyone is roped in to sponsor generously.

PLEASE PITCH IN AND HELP THE

Edridge Benevolent Fund

Lord Hunt, Napo President

1984

Napo was accepted as a member of the TUC. This had been Napo's policy since the 1976 AGM but was only achieved after several years of negotiation.

1984

The Statement of National Objectives and Priorities (SNOP) was published. It was the first centrally imposed definition of what the 56 Probation Areas should be doing. It emphasised that the central purpose of probation was to supervise offenders in the community and that the principal statutory task was the provision of Social Enquiry Reports, the supervision of non-custodial orders including probation and community service, through-care and after-care, in addition to civil work.

1987

Napo endorsed the case for ethnic monitoring. The process was to involve both staff and caseloads.

Napo AGM, 1985

Lobby against training proposals, 1995

1987

The Home Office Green Paper 'Supervision and Punishment in the Community' was published. It proposed electronic monitoring, an idea vigorously opposed by Napo.

1988

A major lobby of Parliament protesting at Home Office plans to move probation away from advising and assisting to community punishment was attended by over 1,000 staff. The meeting was addressed by many MPs, including Paul Boateng and Keith Vaz.

1988

The National Association of Asian Probation Officers (NAAPS) was established to provide a support group of members promoting an Asian perspective on professional issues.

1989

Napo balloted members for industrial action over Home Office demands for a swift response to requests for court reports. The action involved declining new work and referring it back to management.

Protest against the 'Howard Gap', 1986

1991

Napo embarked on its first major concerted industrial action over unsocial hours. The action led to talks and a financial offer which was accepted by members in a 2 to 1 majority.

1991

The Government introduced the Criminal Justice Act. It gave the service a central role in delivering punishment in the community. Probation became a sentence of the court although consent was still required. In addition Social Enquiry Reports were replaced by Pre-Sentence Reports. The Act introduced a revised sentencing framework that was based upon just deserts, that is that the punishment should fit the crime. The concept of seriousness was used to differentiate between those

1912-1987

**NAPO
75th AGM
and
Conference**

PROGRAMME

The Aberconwy Centre
LLANDUDNO
22-25 October 1987

offences that were suitable for a community sentence and those that should result in custody. The combination order was also introduced.

1992

National Standards first introduced in 1988 were substantially revised. They were introduced for all persons under supervision in the community and post-release licenses. They were revised again in 1995, 2000, 2002 and 2005, each time becoming increasingly restrictive on enforcement and by 2000 required staff, for the first time, to propose custody in court reports. This changed one of the fundamental values of the service, that is – dealing with individuals in the community.

1995

Napo held two major lobbies of Parliament when the Home Secretary sought to abolish probation training. Both events were attended by around 1,300 members. Amongst those addressing the conference were MPs Tony Benn, Jack Straw and Margaret Hodge. An Early Day Motion in Parliament sponsored by Napo calling for training to stay in higher education attracted the support of 233 MPs.

Tony Benn MP, 1995

1997

The Probation and Prisons Review was announced. It suggested a regional structure under which service delivery would be improved by greater professionalism and authority at a national level. The same year saw the introduction of 'Effective Practice', 'What Works' and 'Accredited Programmes'.

1998

The Government decided not to merge Prison and Probation following a suggestion to do so the previous year.

1998

The Crime and Public Order Act introduced anti-social behaviour orders, parenting orders, crime and disorder partnerships and home detention curfews.

1999

Napo embarked on a comprehensive workloads campaign involving refusal to take on new work because of excessive caseloads. It led to the development of the Joint Agreement on Priorities and Employee Care with management and the Home Office. Youth Offender Teams were introduced.

2000

The National Probation Service for England and Wales was established under the Criminal Justice and Court Services Act. It commenced work on 1 April 2001 when the 54 Areas were reduced to 42 and 100% funding was introduced by Central Government. This signalled the end of the Probation Service's responsibility for civil work and a separate organisation the Children and Family Court Advisory and Support Service (CAFCASS) was established. The Act also changed the name of probation orders to community rehabilitation orders, community service orders became community punishment orders, and the combination order became the community punishment and rehabilitation order. Napo supported the changes to the structure but not the changes of name. A statutory duty was placed on local Probation Boards to work with victims of crime. They were required to consult and notify victims about the release arrangements of all offenders convicted of a sexual or violent offence which led to a sentence of 12 months or more.

2001

Napo opted to change its title to 'Napo – the trade union and professional association for family court and probation staff'. The move followed the creation of two national services and reflected the changing nature of the union membership.

2001

The National Probation Directorate standardised all the service's work and introduced a common, 'efficient and effective offender risk and needs assessment' known as OASys. The aim of OASys was to underpin the 'What Works' practice and had a pivotal role in assessment. Napo criticised the move as attacking the professionalism of staff.

2003

The Sexual Offences Act introduced Sexual Offences Prevention Orders, Foreign Travel Orders and strengthened the provision of the Sex Offenders Register which was enacted in 1997.

2004

The Government published a response to the Carter Report, 'Managing Offenders, Reducing Crime: A New Approach', entitled 'Reducing Crime: Changing Lives'. This gave support to the creation of a National Offender Management Service and proposed the end-to-end management of offenders.

2004

The Government subsequently announced its intention to introduce privatisation and competition into the delivery of supervision. The effect of the proposals would be to abolish the National Probation Service and introduce fragmentation. Napo commenced a high profile campaign of opposition. An Early Day Motion in the House of Commons attracted 251 signatories from all political parties.

2005

The National Disabled Staff Support Group was established and held its first annual conference in November.

2005

The Criminal Justice Act 2003 was partially implemented including a generic community sentence. Community punishment was as a consequence renamed 'unpaid work'. The key feature of the Act was that the sentence imposed must be proportionate and commensurate with the level of seriousness of the offence. The Act also introduced intermittent and indeterminate custody. The proposals for a new sentence of custody plus, which would replace prison sentences of less than 12 months, and lead to short-term offenders being supervised in the community, was proposed but subsequently dropped in 2006.

2006

The Government introduced a parliamentary Bill to allow for private sector involvement in offender supervision and to reduce local accountability. The move drew opposition from Napo, the PBA and members of the judiciary.

napo

STOP THE NOMS BILL!

The Government is publishing a National Offender Management Bill. If enacted it will effectively abolish the National Probation Service and open it up for private sector involvement. In addition the Government wishes to change Probation Boards into business-like Trusts to help this to happen.

Napo believes that this would have disastrous consequences for offender supervision, public protection and local accountability. It will be urging all MPs to vote against key clauses in the Bill which will give the Secretary of State the power to commission probation services, take away the local accountability of Probation Boards and fragment the Service.

www.napo.org.uk

Photo © Stefano Cagnoni

KEEP PROBATION PUBLIC

NATIONAL ASSOCIATION of
Probation Officers.

Honorary Secretary: G. H. WARNER. *Office: TOWN HALL, CROYDON.*

No. 1   APRIL, 1913.   Price One Penny.

First Meeting of E...

EDITORIAL.

I have for the moment undertaken the position of this journal. I am guiltless of experience in literary matters. I accept, so to speak, for the breach. In due course I trust our journal may be able to enlist the editor of experience. For the present I must trust...

The issue of any periodical small of tremendous anxiety on financial and other grounds, periodical for no purpose whatever of gain upon a different basis. Our anxiety is that shall be helpful to all engaged in probation the volumes will be made full use of for all may further the easier we have at heart and the rank and file.

It is not intended at present to go in any to the date of the issue of probable future date must depend upon the material thus in publication. I hope to receive from time to time and information of interest from probation officers and it is fortunately in a position to state that such has been found in different areas who have...

N.A.P.O.
NEWSLETTER

An occasional bulletin of information for Probation Officer Members issued by the National Association of Probation Officers, 6 Endsleigh Street, London, WC1

No. 1   JANUARY 1965

...SLETTER (replacing NAPO NOTES) now appears in a new for...led in the Report of the Ad Hoc Committee on the Journal whic...at the Edinburgh Conference in 1963. The Report recommende...nal news-sheet should be used for the information of probatio...rs and Branches, and should include much material at prese...circulars. "It should be the main internal source of communicatio...Association and its members on all affairs concerning th...

...ETTER will appear when needed and will sometimes be distribute...nal information, sometimes (as in this instance) alone. It will inclu...obituaries, honours, matters for discussion by Branches, notic...rest, and Branch news. *IT IS MEANT TO BE READ and USE...S and BRANCHES.* The current issue is devoted mainly to matt...embers. Constitutional changes may not seem important f...in voting and in organisation are essential to the developme...tic, professional body and we hope the proposals herein w...ied by Branches and members.

...IONS The Constitution states that subscriptions are due on...are grateful to the many members who have already paid — usua...der. At the same time we can feel only dismayed that 150 memb...e enjoyed a full year of membership (in which they received...

napo news

THE BULLETIN OF THE NATIONAL ASSOCIATION OF PROBATION OFFICERS   JULY 1988 ◆ NUMBER 1

NEW CS STANDARDS ANNOUNCED

Amid a flurry of publicity, around the time of the Spring Bank Holiday, the Home Office published the second draft of its proposed national standards for community service. Launching the standards John Patten said, "These standards are intended to toughen up Community Service. We want the courts and the public to be confident that offenders given Community Service Orders will not find them a soft or easy option and will repay the community for the damage they have done. I think it will be particularly apt if offenders do work actually to improve the appearance of neighbourhoods, including those which they themselves have damaged or vandalised."

The Home Office intends to introduce these standards by 1st January 1989, through a mixture of statutory rules and guidance. Home Office officials will consult the probation service organisations on draft rules and a draft circular. It is not clear how much scope exists for further modification but ministers are clearly determined to impose these standards which they see as part of their 'punishment in the community' initiative.

NAPO submitted a detailed paper attacking the first draft (PR 22/88). This second...

◆ rules governing lateness, sickness and failure to attend have been relaxed slightly, giving the supervisor a little more discretion

◆ the breach rule has been modified to allow the SPO to issue a final warning instead of automatic breach after two failures

The proposed rule governing travelling time has been worsened; it will not now count at all and the guarantee of a maximum journey time to work has been dropped.

These changes have not addressed NAPO's main criticism. The draft standards still favour manual work in groups and threaten the viability of individual placements with voluntary organisations engaged in social service work with disadvantaged groups. The rules will introduce...

new rigidities into CS, making schemes bureaucratic and inflexible. They remove discretion from the probation service and will make CS unworkable for many of the disorganised offenders the scheme now handles. The proposed rules will produce many more breaches on minor, technical grounds including some which may be difficult to prove in court. Inundating the court with breaches will succeed more in weakening confidence in the scheme and...

News . . . 2   Training . . . 8   Black Workers Conference . . . 11

napo NEWS

JUNE 1998   ISSUE 100

CRAMS- PUT YOUR SAFETY FIRST
Detailed advice is carried inside on how members should put their own safety first in line with health and safety legislation, in using CRAMS software. See Page 10

---

napo news

December/January 2007
Issue 185
www.napo.org.uk

Reid undermines Probation
Page 3

Probation Centenary 1907-2007 Probation 2007 Page 7

Prison over-crowding Page 8

Stop the Bill – we can do it!

Over 250 Napo members from across England and Wales were at Westminster last month to lobby MPs on the Bill to privatise Probation. The Offender Management Bill, published as expected on 23 November, will effectively break up the National Probation Service replacing it with a fragmented competitive market.

Lobbyists, crowded into the largest committee room in the House of Commons, applauded MPs and Peers who promised support for Napo's campaign. Many were also able to meet their local MPs to argue the case for opposition to the Bill.

MPs were told that the key Clauses in the Bill are 2, 3 and 4. Clauses 2 and 3 give the Secretary of State the power to take over commissioning from local Boards and pave the way for privatisation. Clause 4 abolishes Probation Boards and replaces them with

business-like Trusts. No business case has been made for the privatisation of Probation, and the NOMS structures remain in a chaotic state.

Justification

Ministers originally claimed that the privatisation agenda was being pursued because the Probation Service was failing. But the Service is performing better than ever according to the Government's own figures produced in August 2006.

Ministers then said that re-offending rates were unacceptably high at 60% and virtually no different from prison. In fact the latest statistics show that prison has a 66% reconviction rate after 2 years compared with 53% for Probation (see page 2).

Napo's response

In a press statement Napo said: "This Bill will, if implemented, lead to the abolition of the National Probation Service and its

replacement with a competitive market. Local accountability would be lost, information sharing between agencies will be diminished by competition, and public protection compromised. The Bill is not about improving standards, it is about privatisation, yet to date no business case has been produced by the Government to show how the replacement of Probation by a market will actually work and improve the delivery of service. Whole probation Areas could be sold off under the arrangements, including the supervision of high risk offenders.

Stop Bill

Lobbying against the Bill began in earnest last month with the launch of Napo's Stop the Bill campaign. Since then, hundreds of members have written to or emailed their local MPs; around 100 MPs have met

Continued on page 2

...arnt that a new e offenders is to be...ater this year. The e voice recognition...one user location...rking would be a...s on parole and...offender or parolee...erious times each...

e have agreed that ll be able to use the wing the signing of ont with the present tests. There have rials in the USA. The offender would he court to carry dicated pager and vected according to e and on a random ffender would then contractor via a re, in accordance weekly monitoring e contractor would

then have the responsibility to ensure that the offender complied with the agreed schedule and would also have responsibility for double checking their whereabouts following random checks.

The detailed daily schedule would include the offender's new place of work, drugs clinic, group sessions, psychiatrists or any other location that was thought appropriate. The day is likely to be highly structured. The new system will be piloted primarily with sex offenders and also those who are receiving drugs and are commonly at risk. The system will be used in conjunction with probation or parole supervision and will be funded through the private sector.

If the offender is not where they should be the contractor investigates immediately and if not satisfied with the offenders explanation can order that they be breached and taken back to court. It is thought that the system will be introduced later this year

when technical problems have been resolved. Currently the voice recognition system only registers American prisoners based in the...

The Kent source said: The system is based on an electronic chip which only recognises the voice. Once it would be resolved during trials was the seat of order to recognise Kent and indeed accents. The system has been put up by private manufacturers and agreed by the Home Office.

In a press statement, NAPO said: "All the research evidence shows that the more contact that offenders have with a probation officer the less likely the public that the voice recognition system is yet another form of privatisation. The cost to private profits rather to proper in hand the Probation Service not to plug gaps through using private companies. The risks must be carefully monitored to see if they do indeed offer value for money."

Harry Fletcher

The changing face of Napo News

Probation Service Values

The role of the Probation Service has changed enormously since its inception and particularly in the last 20 years. Throughout this period Napo members have sought to ensure that the value base of the service has remained the same and that it should always underpin good practice:

'Good quality practice is that which seeks firstly to identify the real causes of offending, to empower the individual to bring about lasting change in her or his circumstances and to find out ways to influence the external factors contributing to her or his behaviour, carried out in a manner which respects the freedom and dignity of the individual at all times'

Napo's Good Practice Guide, 1995

A Probation Values statement is currently displayed in the offices of many Napo members. In celebration of the centenary it was redrafted by Napo's Professional Committee in 2006. The Statement says:

NAPO RECOGNISES THE DAMAGE DONE TO COMMUNITIES AND THE HARM DONE TO INDIVIDUALS BY THE COMMISSION OF CRIME. THE PROBATION SERVICE HAS AN IMPORTANT ROLE TO PLAY IN PROTECTING THE PUBLIC BY WORKING WITH THOSE SENTENCED BY THE COURTS AND THEIR VICTIMS. MUCH CRIME HAS ITS ORIGINS IN SOCIAL INJUSTICE. NAPO KNOWS THAT MANY OF THOSE WHO COMMIT OFFENCES HAVE THEIR LIFE OPPORTUNITIES CURTAILED BY POVERTY, DISCRIMINATION AND SOCIAL EXCLUSION AND HAVE THEMSELVES BEEN VICTIMS OF CRIME.

NAPO BELIEVES THAT PEOPLE ARE CAPABLE OF CHANGING THEIR BEHAVIOURS AND ATTITUDES FOR THE BENEFIT OF THEMSELVES, THEIR FAMILIES AND THE COMMUNITIES IN WHICH THEY LIVE. THEREFORE NAPO AFFIRMS ITS COMMITMENT TO THE FOLLOWING PROBATION VALUES:

- BUILDING SAFER COMMUNITIES THROUGH A LOCAL, PUBLIC AND ACCOUNTABLE PROBATION SERVICE

- PROMOTING SOCIAL JUSTICE AND SOCIAL INCLUSION TO COUNTERACT DISADVANTAGE AND DISCRIMINATION

- RESPECTING AND VALUING THE INDIVIDUAL WHILST CHALLENGING CRIMINAL BEHAVIOUR

- PROVIDING A PROFESSIONAL SERVICE ROOTED IN RATIONAL AND EVIDENCE BASED APPROACHES

- TREATING PEOPLE FAIRLY AND OPENLY ACCORDING TO THEIR INDIVIDUAL NEEDS

NAPO IS COMMITTED TO CHALLENGING AND RAISING AWARENESS OF PRACTICES WHICH IMPACT NEGATIVELY UPON INDIVIDUALS' HUMAN RIGHTS AND THEIR ABILITY TO CHANGE FOR THE BETTER.

Oral histories
Part one

Jill Tibbits

Jill Tibbits started working for the Probation Service in 1951 in Nottinghamshire. She finished her career over 30 years later as Chief Officer for Surrey. During her time she was an active Napo member and was Chair of the union from 1969 to 1972. She now lives in Puddletown in Dorset.

On offenders: 'Realistically offenders included some of the most disadvantaged and damaged people in society, and to try and integrate them back into society was hard. It was costly, but nevertheless it was a lovely job. In my time we learned a lot from CCETSU (Central Council for Education and Training in Social Work). We went on courses and we learned so many things that we really didn't know before.'

On working in Surrey: 'Working in Surrey was great. We were involved in so many new things with people on probation. We formed a care trust. We were able to make phone calls to employers, help people get jobs, that was what probation was all about. We had a landladies scheme on call. Certainly the service was doing personal casework but we were moving into the world outside. Whether the service can keep on doing that into the future I really don't know. We ran an Attendance Centre. The aim was not punitive, but above all to try to give the young people a place in the world eventually. I think it was the first and only attendance centre run by probation. It was a great success because it was based on partnership.'

On offending: 'People will only cease to offend and replace it with something better if they feel you care enough about them. One of the difficulties was that some staff only did reports and nothing else and were cut off from having real relationships with clients. We had to build up individual relationships and relationships with the public.'

On the evolving service: 'There is this view that nothing is effective, and it isn't true. I am surprised really about how many people have actually said "this worked". The Probation Service wasn't nine to five in my day, now it's much more like that. Clients were excluded young people and they still are, nothing changes.'

John Carter Stroud, Gloucestershire

John Carter joined the Probation Service in 1971 on Home Office training. He worked in Bristol, Stroud, Gloucester Prison, Cheltenham and was seconded to the Home Office before retiring in January 2004 as Chief Officer for Gloucestershire. John was a member of Napo and served on the local JNC.

On the modern Service:
'One big change which I think is understandable, because there is a change of scene in all aspects of the public sector, is that when I joined there wasn't a lot of evidence of management. You did feel as a probation officer that you were left to get on and do your own thing. Most people did what they thought was a good job. Probation officers were, on the whole, conscientious and worked quite long hours doing the job in the best way they thought. There were no National Standards just a few guidelines. When I started you had meetings with your Senior Probation Officer but you didn't think of them as your manager but more as a casework supervisor. I remember even as a student on placement being told to go and do court duties in Totnes Magistrates' Court for the next four and a half months. Obviously, I had a placement supervisor but it was quite odd to be given so much freedom and responsibility, and actually quite enjoyable. I never complained. It was much less about procedure and process than it is now.'

On achievements: 'There were two I was really pleased about. They were both about the same thing, which was communication and partnership. I did my utmost as a probation officer to form a good relationship with the courts, the front window of the Service. I went to the former case committees, became involved in magistrate training, and then as I went up the management tree I really worked hard at relationships with other court users and sentencers. The second achievement which I worked at was forging links between the Service and other organisations, both statutory and voluntary. For example, as a senior probation officer I piloted joint working with prison staff and helped set-up Victim Support in Cheltenham. At Head Office, I sat on many inter-agency groups including latterly chairing the first countywide Drug and Alcohol Action Committee (DAAT). That was really challenging. It was enjoyable and it was interesting because by the time I left, I felt that the Service had effective working relationships with other agencies and bodies.'

On the current climate: 'When I was seconded to the Home Office, I was concerned how much senior civil servants were reacting on a daily basis to Ministers without considering the implications of policy changes on Probation staff doing the "job". In a way it was outrageous. When I was in London I wanted to say to them "hang on, can you not stand up to the Minister a bit". You know, don't be rude but tell them about the real world. I expect I was seen as an irritation sometimes. An example of a poor policy change was the running of the national Probation estate. Overnight someone said "Probation property across the country is poor, you need much better managed property, you're not running it properly, you're wasting money. Some areas have got good contracts, some areas have poor contracts but we will sweep it altogether and create a national system where everybody pays say £2 per annum per square metre for the property you've got." I said, hang on, the bill has risen by £200,000 a year for Gloucestershire and we now have less local control of what is going on, particularly building maintenance. But it was banging your head against a brick wall because it was the new philosophy of "we do it big". External organisations bidding for these new national contracts did not have the staff to run them, and when they recruited the staff they didn't have the expertise or experience to run the project successfully.'

On bidding and contestability: 'It just seems to me to be an absolute waste of energy and resources which could be redirected to doing the job. I am told that the private prisons have pushed up standards and although I can understand the thinking behind that, I do not agree that this is the only way of improving performance. Maybe you can do something like that with Probation, but if you throw everything out to contestability there is a real risk of failure and demoralising and losing good staff.'

On his contribution: 'My most positive memory was that I felt I was doing something useful. In a civilised society there is a need for a Probation Service. We recognised there was a need for the work we did with offenders rather than just punishing them all or locking them up. When I joined the Service there was an attitude that Probation was the solution to everything but by the time I left we had a more balanced and carefully thought out view recognising the rights of victims as well as offenders. It was good working for an organisation that did something important and useful, particularly being involved in public protection. It was very positive for me.'

'When I talk to people about equal opportunities and diversity, I realise how much attitudes changed during the period of my career and how often the Probation Service was in the forefront of many of these developments. It was good working through them.

My first student supervisor was female. When I joined I was used to coming across females in the Service, but it was more male dominated, although Gloucestershire had a female assistant chief probation officer. I can remember having to persuade a prison governor that it was OK to give female probation officers working in prisons keys whereas he never questioned giving male probation officers keys. This debate would not need to take place now.'

Brian Horner Barnsley, Yorkshire

Brian Horner started work for Probation in 1966, retiring 27 years later in 1989. He was a direct entrant who later went for training at Sheffield University. From 1975 he was a senior probation officer in Greater Manchester, having previously worked as a wool sorter in Bradford. For the last sixteen years he has been the Yorkshire representative for the Edridge Fund. He was the first male officer in Barnsley to supervise a female client.

On joining the service: 'I think Probation bothered about people. You were involved with them, you were trying to make a difference. That's what prompted me to join the service. I have no regrets,

I enjoyed every day, and I have been really fortunate lately as an Edridge rep which keeps me in touch with the service. I regularly attend branch meetings. It was a privilege being involved with people and having them break out of the offending pattern. I loved Family Court Welfare, custody work and children, access and family involvement. In those days we did adoption work in Barnsley. It was ever so rewarding. I was sorry to lose the Family work. There were lots of positive aspects to the job. The autonomy was one thing. Having come from industry where you had to measure output and work by the clock the opportunity to manage your own caseload was marvellous. And another positive thing for me was the court. Court work was the shop front.'

On achievements: 'I advised, assisted and befriended and brought about change. The job was an achievement. Working in the prison with the prison staff I was a member of a team. We had a senior – a woman senior – we felt we were doing something positive. There were no ancillaries. I left before one was appointed. I never thought about it in terms of achievements until thinking about it lately. There was a lot of development work in Wakefield. The regional secure unit was introduced. In my day we had to stand up in court and read reports out. The Adult Court as well as the Juvenile. Often, for some reason, Barnsley Court used to encourage schoolchildren to go into courts, and the officer would be there reading something out and the children would be there listening. It was marvellous work. The Probation Service is value for money. It kept people out of prison. Compare the costs.'

'In 1967 I supervised a female client on a probation order. I was the first male officer in Barnsley to supervise a female. The order ended successfully and the client went on to become a nurse at the local hospital. Shortly after I retired I had to have a bone marrow inspection which was very painful and my former client was the nurse who held my hand during the process.'

Peggy Turner Barnsley, Yorkshire

Peggy Turner joined the Probation Service in 1949. She left in 1953, rejoined again in 1969 having brought up her children, and remained as a main grade officer until 1987. She worked in Derbyshire and in Wakefield and trained at Nottingham University for a Diploma in Social Science, she also studied at Rainer House, in London.

On probation: 'I have always got on with people. It certainly opened my eyes. My parents were head teachers. I didn't want to teach but that's how I'd been brought up, I wanted to do some good. I loved working with people and everybody was so helpful. The police – I mean we worked closely with the police in those days – they were in court a lot and I liked the magistrates. I loved working with clients.'

'I loved the job. With young boys particularly it was pretty hard, getting them to do community service, or getting them on something like a bike mending project, or mechanics. It was good finding a legitimate outlet for their interests. I remember one young man, he was very difficult, I almost gave up but he asked me to carry on, and I carried on seeing him. He was very difficult, he had a lot of anger in him. He was about 20 and I actually brought him to the house at one stage. He came from a reasonable family and was actually quite clever, he went to boarding school. But

Roy and Peggy Turner

I managed to get him into interesting projects and turned him round. I did work with another lad who had an awful background. He'd been abused. In the end we managed to get him to Grendon and I went down to Grendon often on a Saturday to visit him. It worked, it worked a treat.'

On the future: 'I worry about the future. I would like to see more staff visiting people at home. They are much more at ease and they talk much more easily. That's why we did our SERs that way. I never used to call them into the office unless it was absolutely vital. I'd go to their houses and they appreciated it. What worries me now is that that's no longer happening, so how do we get to the heart of these people. In my day, we walked the streets, visiting people. For the future we need to work at getting respect back from magistrates.'

Barbara Streimer West London

Barbara Streimer joined the Probation Service in 1960 following a Home Office sponsored course. Beginning in Yorkshire, she later continued to work in London in various court and community teams, before retiring in October 1990. She was also one of the first probation officers to work in Pentonville. In late 1964 she took a career break and did a seven month tour of the United States, meeting probation officers, judges, going into prisons, meeting families and looking at psychiatric community care. She also chaired the Napo Branch Negotiating Committee in London.

On community involvement: 'In the early '70s I was one of a group of probation officers involved in setting up a day centre for difficult clients referred by other probation officers. We had high-flying ideals. It was wonderful. This was Sherborne House, and we had fantastic training ideas for the clients. It was planned as an egalitarian structure. The idea was that people coming in would have the same rights and opportunities as the people working in it. I suppose it was a bit of an illusion when you think about it, but it was a quite extraordinary setup. Sherborne School in Dorset provided the opportunity for Sherborne House in London to happen.

Unlike Sherborne School we were going to work with people of all ages. It was great. We had a music therapist, we had a kiln in there and a pottery teacher, and we ourselves went through training using a psychologist and a particular form of psychological interaction. We learned a lot. Of course we got into trouble for allowing it to develop the way it did, but we had in there amazing, amazing people. Some of the people who came had a history of violence, but we rarely had violent episodes.'

On the Probation Service: 'I went to all the groups I could and made contributions to Home Office working parties We had wonderful opportunities then. When I look at some of the papers produced I can't believe having played a part. I remember when they started up A and B grades, and I remember going to a big rally in Birmingham. We were very angry about the proposal. I was against it in principle, and I actually spoke at length at the conference and I got very excited about that. There were so many things about the service, the way it provided chances for POs to develop skills, the groups, the involvement with Jean Graham Hall, the child abuse study groups that were run. I was asked if I would train and teach on that. I didn't want to teach. I wanted to be "out there", involved. It was sad that probation officers – and I may be wrong in this – don't seem to get the same opportunities now for various reasons. I am an absolute believer in home visits, because how on earth otherwise can you know what is going on.'

On positive contributions: 'Everything was so beneficial in a way. It gave me such a wide-ranging experience of other people's lives. I was involved with a domestic case and, after she was left to bring up two children on her own, all these years later letters and telephone calls from their mother keep we informed of their remarkable achievements in life. It was so important being prepared to take on people no-one else would take: being prepared not to judge them because they had already been judged.'

On making a difference: 'Of course we didn't to all, but we did to some. I recall a girl in a Juvenile Court who had been seen by a psychiatrist who wanted to see her father, but he refused to cooperate. He never came to court with her and wasn't there when a supervision order was made, so I took her home. We found her father and stepmother sitting on two chairs side by side, one of them holding a small brown paper bag. I didn't know what to do. We just left when it was clear they wouldn't take her in and she would run away again. She broke all the rules, did everything I asked her not to but never lost touch, and never has done to this day. There was a prisoner I worked with over several years, in conjunction with one of the educationalists, who went on to gain the highest university degree possible, and then forge an outstanding career.'

On the future: 'I fear for it as it heads towards privatisation. I feel about the Probation Service that it should never, ever, forget its position as a social casework agency, coupled with an acknowledgement that it is still, and always has been, an imposition of authority through the magistrates courts, and through all courts in fact. You have to combine the two skills and you have to learn that there are rules if you are going to live in a community, otherwise you get out of the community. And the community is what's out there on the streets, which is where I always wanted to be.'

Doug Boxall Sutton, London

Doug Boxall joined the Probation Service as a clerical officer in 1939. He was called up in 1941 and joined the Marine Corps section. In his own words, 'we dashed out into the channel to pick up all the airmen who'd parachuted into the drink, which is what we called it'. On returning from the war he joined the Central After-Care Association and became the only probation officer in the 'Men's Division' visiting prisons across the West Country. He subsequently worked for the Inner London Probation and Aftercare Service.

On probation: 'There weren't all that many people being released in my day. I used to give talks to a crowd of prisoners who were about to be released and tell them what they could expect in the way of aftercare. As a probation officer I would help them get work, accommodation, and other things. I remember doing home visits in Clapham at eight or nine o'clock at night and not once, not once, was I ever accosted by hoodlums. Not in those days.'

On being a main grade officer: 'I was a main grade throughout. I liked to work with people you see. I served Camberwell Green Magistrates' Court and I remember on one occasion Lady Salmon, (wife of the Lord Chief Justice) had a young woman in front of her with her two colleagues. And she said "well I'm going to sentence you to the detention centre". I immediately sprang to my feet before the Clerk had got to his and said, "you can't do that, Madam", "Why, Mr Boxall, can't I do it?", "Because they don't exist", "They don't exist?" Yes, this was a woman and there were no female detention centres in those days, they didn't exist. And the courts they had respect for us, the Probation Service, that's why they remanded people for social enquiry reports, to help them come to some decision as to how to deal with the case. Yes, I used to enjoy the court work too. Sometimes magistrates would put a case back. I would take the person outside and get some idea of their social history and then go back and address the court. I used to like that. Except when it came to finding accommodation, that was difficult. We used church hostels and Salvation Army hostels. There was a Salvation Army hostel in Great Peter Street, not many people know that, not far from the headquarters of the Probation Service.'

Geoffrey Parkinson Sutton, London

Geoffrey Parkinson joined the Probation Service in 1954. He remained a main grade officer throughout the period, working in different parts of London, finally retiring in 1992.

On his early days in Napo: 'Frank Daltry, he was the General Secretary in the '50s, and the central preoccupation within Napo was the death penalty. That was the great discussion point. There was never any discussion about conditions of service. And when people tried to bring in discussion of salaries they were almost, in fact I think they were on one occasion, booed down. You have to realise there were lots of people in the service who had no reason to want an income. They were often the daughters of the very affluent who wanted to fill their time usefully. When the then Chief Officer brought in the idea of keeping some sort of accounts system they felt this was an intrusion into the question of their honesty and they absolutely refused to do it. They thought there was an implication that they weren't doing their job properly.'

On probation: 'I began to look at probation as if you've got an aircraft carrier, when the aircraft lands on the carrier you've got some sort of roping that goes across the carrier. As the aircraft lands on the deck it runs into these ropes and it slows it down. I saw probation as one of the ropes. You didn't have to think of success in terms of one period of probation, it was a sort of package deal in the way you had to think about it. Often I thought, well we haven't stopped him, but you're not going to stop a percentage of them. They're going to have to go through a system and thing is to try and work out which systems work for which individual. Colleagues didn't take that line. They felt if it didn't work once it was a failure. But it wasn't a failure. For me it was all part of a process.'

On the issue of trust: 'Some officers were successful in a limited way by being old colonels. "You get into trouble and I'll see you in court", They had some success, but only some success – that's the snag. I thought of being an "old colonel" if I thought I could pull it off. The offenders had to know that I could be a bastard but I never actually was. I remember a chap who was up in court, there had been a fight on the top of a bus, and a passenger's eye had been knocked out. He was caught and held responsible. I would see him two or three times and have a friendly chat with him. What a nice old geezer he said once of me. And then on the last day I said I want to see you, we're going to have a serious talk. I told him I was going to write a good report on him but he had to promise not to hurt anybody again. If he did I'd come down on him. I never said anything about petty theft, but physical violence or the threat of physical violence, if you do that I'll even come back off my leave and make sure you go down. And believe me he didn't get involved in violence again.'

Sue Wade, Joan McCarthy, Molly Paul, April Chidgey

Hampshire

Sue Wade joined the Probation Service in 1979 as a Probation Officer, before retiring in 2001 as an Assistant Chief Officer. She was Vice-Chair and Secretary of her Napo Branch for many years.

Joan McCarthy joined the Probation Service in 1952 and worked in Devon and Hampshire until she retired in 1982. During her career in the service she joined the Training Inspectorate and was ACO in London and Hampshire.

Molly Paul joined the Probation Service in 1953. She trained at Rainer House, was appointed to the Hampshire Probation Service and worked in the Juvenile Courts in London and a probation hostel in Clapham, before joining the Home Office Inspectorate in 1963. She retired in 1987.

April Chidgey joined the service in 1984 after training at Southampton University. She worked in a probation centre, community service, Winchester Prison and in Family Court Welfare. Although retired she still works occasionally in the Family Courts.

Molly Paul

Joan McCarthy, on joining the service: 'It's a long time ago and so much has happened since – changes of thinking and so forth. There was quite a lot of questioning about my appointment but that usually happens when a main grade officer is made up to Inspector. But I got through alright. It doesn't matter what grade you are as long as you do the job well. I left after about five or six years and went back to Inner London as Assistant Chief before finally retiring from Hampshire in 1982'

April Chidgey, on joining Probation: 'I trained as a mature student at Southampton. In 1984 I was appointed to a Probation Centre because they were starting up then – Schedule 11B, that's right – and I was just talking about this the other day, because we did things then we would never be allowed to get away with now. We had two probation officers and sometimes 30 clients, and we used to do things like take them on trips. I'm still in touch with so many of my colleagues. We had a real team and of course we had some very posh volunteers.'

'In 1987 I went to work in Winchester prison. I was very interested in working with sex offenders. This was all fairly new then so there was lots of arm twisting and talking to very good governors. We had a really good governor who agreed to keep prisoners back to complete a very short sex offender programme, but at least it was a start. It was the beginning of group work. This was way before cognitive behaviour. The Governor, Tim Newell, worked very much together with the psychiatric support there and we really devised the programme ourselves. It was really quite, sort of heady, exciting stuff at the time. Lots of building of trust to enable you to challenge'

Sue Wade, on achievements: 'My main achievement was being able to get on and try new ideas, and develop them, and being given the autonomy to do so. I think that was probably the big thing, and I think for all of us, in different ways. I just sort of disappeared off to social services and set up a new scheme for five years. I had a lot of contact with probation when I was doing that. Setting up a group work programme, setting up crime projects in Portsmouth. All of us, all in different offices, were all interested in getting out and changing the way things were done. I think national standards are fine, it's the thought of national control that worries me. I'm happy with the idea that everybody should come up to a certain standard, but it's killed off enterprise and innovation, I think. You don't get permission nowadays to just take an idea and develop it yourself as a main grade officer.'

Sue Wade

Joan McCarthy, on achievements: 'During the whole of my time in the service I had a lot of satisfaction in that you could do what you wanted to do, although you were up against certain difficulties. There were difficulties with administration and management. Yes I got plenty of pain out of the work but a lot of joy as well.'

Molly Paul, on achievements: 'I can tell you absolutely I wouldn't have missed a whisker of it. It was only really in the end that I began to see that everything was going the wrong way, and I am now absolutely appalled at what we've got. That's not to say there aren't individual things that are going well but I'm deeply concerned over the quality of training of probation officers.'

Joan McCarthy, on the Probation Service: 'I want to say, talking about my time in the Probation Service, the opportunities offered me to broaden my horizons were wonderful. I went to America. I went all over the place with them. And I think I can say without any argument that I grew up in the Probation Service, I went in green and came out all the colours of the rainbow.'

Sue Wade, on the Probation Service: 'I think it's one of the few professions where you get an understanding of the struggle of people to live ordinary lives. I always liked the bit where we were like the buffer between the organised state and people who were on the edges of it and trying to make sense of it.'

Molly Paul, on the Probation Service: 'I'm deeply concerned over the quality of training of probation officers. I first began to realise this in Mental Health Tribunals when probation officers would come to talk about patients. I remember asking one particular officer whether they had any history with reference to a social enquiry report, and she said what do you mean by history? You can imagine the expression on my face. To me that was the end really, and I suppose they didn't know anything about the relationship between clients and their family.'

April Chidgey, on making a difference: 'Joan talked about going in green and coming out all the colours of the rainbow. I think it could apply to everybody. You often don't look at the breakthroughs but occasionally you do get them and I think they are incredibly satisfying. I'll give you an example. It was on the Ocean Youth Training Ships. I sent two lads at separate times on these, and the second lad had very little confidence. I had to take him down to Gosport in my car, which would probably be against all health and safety regulation these days. He kept saying, "I'm not going, I'm not bloody going". I said you are! He was lonely and frightened and I thought to myself what should I do? Later he contacted me to say he'd been seasick and wanted to come home. I said just stick with it, and when I met him two weeks later he was a different guy. He'd made amazing progress, it was great. I got a letter from him seven years later telling me he'd made quite a success of himself and I just thought that was brilliant.'

April Chidgey

Sue Wade, on casework: 'I remember a typical Portsmouth family. I had three of them on probation at one time – mum, dad and the daughter. The son had managed to escape with a conditional discharge. They were serial shoplifters. I got them because the court had got fed up with thinking of anything else to do with them. And in a way that was what probation was sometimes used by the courts, for people when they didn't know what to do. I don't think these days they would be high enough risk to get anywhere near us but they used to come in regularly. The mother would come in with a big stack of bills and we'd go through them each week and work out her income. It was all pretty chaotic. They were actually good musicians. They were up at night-time and asleep in the day, so the chances of them ever getting a decent job were zero. I had three probation orders in a row on these people, but eventually I got them to stop shoplifting because it was getting them into great difficulties and got their income straight, and got them the benefits to which they were entitled. Later they were charged with stealing electricity by feeding the meter with coins. I kept working with them, it was almost like a family conference, and got them back on another probation order for three years. The judge accepted my view that progress was being made, that something had happened, and that there was a chance that they would turn round and lead law abiding lives. I think that because somebody – me – had listened to what they said, from that day they didn't commit any other offences. Of course they struggled but they coped.'

Joan McCarthy

Molly Paul, on women and children: 'When I started the age of criminal responsibility was eight. Women officers were only allowed to supervise women and children. We could supervise juvenile girls but only boys up to the age of eleven. It was a real breakthrough when that changed. However, during my time I never, ever supervised men.'

Joan McCarthy, on dress codes: 'I do remember when we went to court we all had to wear the office hat. When I was in Plymouth the office hat did the rounds. You had to have a jacket and a hat.'

Sue Wade, on dress codes: 'We had a jacket on the back of the door as well as the office hat. The weird thing was this was the late '70s so men would be dressed in '70s flares. We had one guy with a medallion and clogs and things. Yet the women were still wearing a hat in court. We said hang on a bit this is discrimination. There didn't seem to be a dress code for men but there was definitely a dress code for women. Though I must say we had one or two cool characters who liked strolling in in hippy stuff and they didn't get the respect. And remember you used to have to get permission if you didn't have the proper clothes. You had to go into court to creep before the Magistrates and ask the clerk if it was OK to be in court not in proper dress. You were caught out if you were called to court suddenly and you then had to apologise.'

April Chidgey, on court anecdotes: 'A story I remember at Crown Court was not long ago. A High Court Judge, terribly prim and proper, and sort of looking over the top of his glasses. It was a drugs trial and there was a conspiracy and quite a lot of complicated evidence. And there was this letter that the jury had heard, I think it was a transcript of telephone call that the prison had obviously intercepted. And the jury wanted to hear the letter again. The judge said he was prepared to read the letter to the court to save time. So he said "Yo there! Rude boy, how you doing?" We just sat there, we couldn't move for laughing, it was so incongruous.'

Sue Wade, on the service: 'I think people still go into the service for the same reasons. I don't detect anything else. I think they want to make a difference. They can see that there's a need. I think the ability of those individuals to do something different has been pretty much curtailed though. There is a lot more conformity than there used to be. Conformity that means you can expect a minimum standard of service is good. I've got no objection to the users of the service being happy to be able to receive a sort of minimum standard. Conformity when it means you can't follow your instincts though, and do something because you know that that's going to be the right thing to do, I think is not good news.'

April Chidgey, on the service: 'There has been a shift in how the public perceive probation. I think there's tremendous expectation. You only have to look at what's happening in the press, where probation is being pilloried. I think it reflects the expectation that people have of the Health Service, where everything has a cure, and it's almost like a probation officer should be perfect. They're letting them out of prison with the expectation that the probation officer is with them 24 hours a day preventing them from doing anything bad, but they are missing the bit about personal responsibility and the fact that at the end of the day people will do what they do.'

Doreen Kenyon and Delia Zeuthen

Solihul, Birmingham

Delia Zauthen

Doreen Kenyon worked for the Probation Service from 1957 to 1982. She was a main grade and a Senior Probation Officer in the Birmingham Service, and then in 1974 it became part of the West Midlands. She believes she was one of the first female seniors appointed in 1974.

Delia Zeuthen, as a qualified teacher, was appointed as a direct entrant in 1963. From 1967 to 1974 she was a Student

Supervisor in Birmingham Probation. She was the first woman to work in Winston Green Prison. She stayed as a main grade officer throughout her career until retiring in 1990.

Delia Zeuthen, on joining probation: 'Mr Worthy was the Chief Probation Officer. My ex-husband was Danish. I had come back from Denmark and my qualification as a teacher took me in. I appeared before the full probation committee wearing my hat and coat but nobody wanted me because I was divorced. In fact if it hadn't been for Mr Worthy standing up for me I don't think I would have been appointed.'

Delia Zeuthen, on the service: 'At one time I had a full caseload of 50 and two days off a week to do in-service training. I was always interested in students. I was one of the few who never got the CQSW. In 1968 I was asked to go into Winston Green Prison. I was the first woman to go into the nick. The Chief said if it didn't work I could come out after 6 months. They put me in the remand wing. I arrived on the same day as the dogs. They were not sure who was going to cause the most trouble me or the dogs. I think it was me.'

Doreen Kenyon, on joining probation: 'I think I enjoyed the challenge. I enjoyed working with offenders particularly, and I suppose I also enjoyed the drama of the court if I'm honest. And the other thing that attracted me was that each day was unpredictable, you never knew what was going to happen next.'

Delia Zeuthen, on the service: 'I never regretted going into Probation, but it was working with people that I wanted to do. It was never the same, you never knew what was going to happen when you walked into the office. That was what interested me, and where you were going to be and what you were going to be doing. That's why I stayed, but I was glad when I left because it was not what I'd come to do. It was reading bits of paper. But I so enjoyed the earlier part.'

Doreen Kenyon, on making a difference: 'I was always brought up to believe that you should view the whole situation, not totally the offender or totally the community. But I believe if society and the law demanded that somebody went to prison it was my job in the end to prepare them for what could happen. That they could go to prison for some sorts of offences and it was my job to support them and their family through it.'

Delia Zeuthen, on a vocation: 'I cared about the client. I would always say this, but I did care about them. And I think they knew this, I think they knew I cared about them, but they knew there was a line beyond which they couldn't go. I said these are the boundaries that we have to work in and I support you all the way, if it doesn't work, tough! I have always felt this – we have got boundaries. I was brought up with boundaries and felt this is what the job is all about. But maybe this is old fashioned.'

Delia Zeuthen, on achievements: 'I remember one prisoner, as he was the most awkward customer, and he was handed to me. He hadn't really been seen. Nobody had visited him in prison. Eventually he came out and he was on parole and he would ring me up and say he couldn't come in because he hadn't got any money to come on the bus. So I'd tell him to walk. And he did walk, actually, and it worked. We got on, we had a relationship. He was difficult but I persevered, and I remember two years later, when I was working somewhere else, they said he'd come in to see me and I said send him up. He'd come to tell me that he'd got a flat in town, in Birmingham, he'd got a job and he asked me would I have tea with him. Everybody said you shouldn't go because he was so troublesome. But I went to see him and he told me he was chuffed that somebody had bothered to work with him and come to see his new flat and his job. I must admit I thought as soon as he'd finished probation he would be back in crime and inside, but he wasn't.'

Doreen Kenyon, on supervision: 'When I started out I was only allowed to supervise women and young children. I wasn't allowed to supervise men in the beginning. Indeed we weren't even on equal pay when I joined. What I supervised was mainly youngsters, shoplifters. I remember one shoplifter I had, she'd never let me visit her at home. I tried and tried, and this was a great learning curve for me because she was eventually charged with defrauding social security because she'd got a husband at home. And she was the first woman I'd ever supervised who went to prison and that had a galvanising effect on me.'

Doreen Kenyon

Doreen Kenyon, on making a difference: 'I'm sure we made a difference. We enabled them to talk for one thing, and to communicate. I think that is obviously one of the things that breaks down a relationship, breaks down families, communication goes. And we showed them we cared. We were someone who took an interest in them, and in their situation, and tried to help them change. And also in my day we didn't have targets. Although I suppose we did have targets in one way – they looked to see how many home visits you'd done and how many office visits you'd received. I suppose in a loose sort of way they were targets and you were measured on it. But I know now there are loads of targets and form filling and what have you.

Doreen Kenyon, on team spirit. 'In our day everybody was supportive. It was a family atmosphere. I can remember when a colleague of ours was in a road crash and his wife was killed and he was in hospital with his three children miles away. We were able to ring up the probation office near where the hospital was and they went to see him and visited him. I can't imagine that happening these days. There was a sort of family feeling throughout the probation service, and each year we all met up at the Napo conference and networked and formed links.'

Delia Zeuthen, on team spirit: 'There was a very strong support system in Birmingham when we first started. I look back, and they carried me, or they must have done for at least six months. I was floundering during that time, but everybody was so supportive.'

Delia Zeuthen, on making a difference: 'We did make a change when we went into Winston Green as a group of probation officers. I'm sure we did begin to change the outlook of the prison staff and they changed towards us. Because you could feel at first they didn't want us in and they weren't going to cooperate. But it changed. Winston Green then was a remand prison and also they only stayed there if they were serving short sentences. It was a fluid group of people but I think we made a difference.'

Doreen Kenyon, on the future: 'I don't know about the future. I would like to hope there is a place for probation, that we can help people change their lives. But we seem to have got into a blame culture, and we're in a situation where it's going to be more difficult to take risks because there's so much blame being laid at the Probation Service's door, especially with people on parole. I mean how the public expects the Probation Service to supervise people 24 hours a day when they come out on parole is nobody's business. I mean they ought to be looking at how people are paroled.'

Delia Zeuthen, on the service: 'If it's true what they say now that people are talking to people on the phone for parole reports, and by video link, I find this appalling. I mean, I don't see how you could interview somebody like that. I think you do need to see somebody face to face. But now that doesn't happen. They don't go down and do home visits for a report. If this is true, if you just see people at the office and not at home, I'm worried. In our day you got shouted at if you didn't do home visits. Something else that's changed is that in my day it was always Mrs Kenyon and Mrs Zeuthen, it was never Christian names. But I'm told that happens today with a lot of clients. I feel you have to put the boot in sometimes and if you're on Christian name terms it makes it harder. I mean maybe it's just a small thing.'

Joyce Rimmer Kingsheath, Birmingham

Joyce Rimmer worked as a main grade probation officer between 1956 and 1963. She then worked in Birmingham University until 1990, training probation officers in the Diploma in Social Work and Social Science Masters in the Department of Social Administration.

On joining the service: 'I read history at Bristol and became very interested in 19th century social history, and particularly women in prisons and Elizabeth Fry, and I thought if I join the Probation Service I might be able to do something about keeping women out of prison. I never succeeded, and of course it's worse now than it ever was then. But I got a place at LSE to do a Certificate in Social Science. I then got a job for a year at the Shaw Approved School in Warrington, a classifying school for girls, a horrendous place. I worked there for almost a year and lost 4 stones. The only time you ever got out was when they absconded and you had to drive the Ford Popular to go and pick them up at the police station, and get bonked on the head by the girls. I was 22 years old when I was doing that.'

On achievements: 'I like to think that most of the people that we supervised on probation didn't re-offend. I mean it was pretty rare to go back to breach somebody and pretty rare to have a supervision order go wrong, because we gave them social work help and I knew more or less why the people I supervised were in trouble, and we did something about the causes. I gave them help. I advised, assisted and befriended, and I gave them a lot of befriending. I knew about their matrimonial problems, I knew about their worries over the children. I gave them an interview like a counsellor might give them now.'

'I think people looked up to probation officers. The magistrates looked up to probation officers and depended a lot on their opinions, and we had a professional status in the courts. That changed after, the whole of social work changed, after Seebohm. Everything changed after Seebohm. In my opinion it went terribly wrong in 1970.'

On making a difference: 'Well, If people couldn't read and write you made sure they got some help with learning to read and write. And if they hadn't got a job you helped them to get enough confidence to get a job. We rehabilitated people. And of course we did an awful lot of matrimonial work.'

'I was 24 and I was listening to husbands and wives arguing with one another. What did I know about it? I was there, and they were

talking, and that was the main thing. And lots of people that I had on Probation, I think, well I'm sure, they'd never had a conversation with an adult for half an hour before. And if you listened to them for half an hour that was the best thing you could do.'

On the future: 'I don't know. I despair of it. I don't know what this Government is doing. The Justice policy is an absolute mess. The prisons can't do their job because they're too full. I listen to it all, I read it all in the paper, I don't know what the answers are. I get Christmas cards from former students and some of them say, "I've left. I can't take it any more". And some say, "this is such a hard job, I don't know how long I can go on". They're supervising lifers all the time, and things like that. I don't know. I'm just glad I'm not teaching them now. Because I wouldn't want to think about the future.'

On protection: 'There were 30 probation officers in Birmingham when I came in and just 3 of them women. A lot of the girls were on supervision for moral danger, as it was called then, care and protection. And they weren't trivial because some of them were pregnant anyway. The school attendance cases, they made me cross, because it looked as though the school attendance officers were just bringing them to court in order to get ticks for their boxes, and you know they got credit because they picked up so many non-attenders. Now if they'd been proper social workers they wouldn't have done that, they'd have worked with them. So there was no need for any of these school attendance cases. Yet at one time I had 40 of them.'

'But I look back and I think the thing I've always appreciated was how kind every probation officer was to one another. I've never seen it in the same way with social workers. Always, we literally shared our troubles. We all did this. We'd always go to one another's houses, and these days funerals. There was a great camaraderie. They were a marvellous crowd. But soon there'll be hardly anybody left to go to the funerals.'

Probation in film and television

'This boy has had a difficult time at home, where the moral influence is not good, he has mixed with a set of youths, some of whom have police records, but he regrets what has happened quite sincerely and I feel certain that it will not happen again. Any confidence placed in him now would be justified. I believe in him.'

Ernest Jay as a Magistrate in
'I believe in you'

'I was puzzled to begin with, disheartened and then exasperated.'

Cecil Parker as Phipps in
'I believe in you'

'Feet, sore feet, blistered feet, wet feet, cold feet, thus were the days and seasons marked in those first months as a Probation Officer. They took me to places I'd never heard of, places I never knew existed.'

Cecil Parker as Phipps in
'I believe in you'

'You know I could have taken you back to court for this, but for some unknown reason I believe in you.'

Cecil Parker as Phipps to
Hooker played by Harry
Fowler

'Well Johnstone! You have behaved very foolishly, but your Probation Officer thinks you are genuinely sorry. I will give you another chance. I will put on one year's Probation to Mr Phipps, who will advise, assist and befriend you.'

Godfrey Teale as a Magistrate in
'I believe in you'

'It's no good planning FOR people, you have to plan WITH them.'

Celia Johnson as Matty in
'I believe in you'

'I have heard what the Probation Officer says of you, she believes in you.'

Godfrey Teale as a Magistrate in
'I believe in you'

'A Probation Officer's life is full of disappointments.'

Celia Johnson as Probation Officer Matty in
'I believe in you'

After his first exhausting day as a probation officer, during which he has tramped many miles visiting his probationees and families, Phipps soaks his weary feet in a bowl of water and contrives to regain some of the Duke Street elegance in his shoes. I Believe in You, 1950

Scarce as they are in film, television and literature, (compared to police, lawyers, prosecutors, judges and even prison staff), the various post-war media representations of probation officers do shed a little light on probation's history. In *Good Time Girl* (1948), a woman probation officer in twin set and a fetching little hat briefly reads out a social enquiry report in a juvenile court to stern magistrate Flora Robson. This was one of a number of social realist movies made in Britain in the aftermath of WW2. In Ealing Studio's *I Believe in You* (1950), the probation officer took centre stage. Mr. Phipps (Cecil Parker) was a middle aged former Colonial Officer newly returned from Africa, wondering what uses his skills might be put to, who finds himself separating the incorrigible from the redeemable in South London (among them youngsters Lawrence Harvey and Joan Collins). He imbibes the spirit of probation from his missionary-esque old senior, eventually takes over from him, and falls in love with the lady probation officer Matty (Celia Johnson).

The Ealing ethos, with a slightly harder edge, passed into television in a 1959-62 ATV series called *Probation Officer*, set in and supported by the London Probation Service. Sincere and realistic in its portrayal of efforts to rehabilitate young offenders, it gave an early starring role to Honor Blackman as probation officer Iris Cope. John Stroud's (1961) novel *Touch and Go* was a somewhat despondent counterpoint to the TV series' idealism; his probation officer gives up on the intractable delinquents in a Stevenage-like new town, and moves to more satisfying work... in Ludlow. He was nonetheless a better chap than the vindictive Mr Deltoid, the probation officer supervising young Alex in Anthony Burgess's (1962) novel *A Clockwork Orange*, and played to sleazy perfection in Stanley Kubrick's 1971 film.

In this revealing crime drama adapted from Arthur La Bern's novel 'Night Darkens the Street' Jean Kent has a role of an ambitious girl who becomes a criminal, mainly through her unfortunate environment
Good Time Girl, 1948

'Don't let it get you down' Matty whispers to Phipps. It is his first appearance in court as a PO and he is unprepared for the sarcasm of the presiding magistrate. I Believe in You, 1950

Honor Blackman who starred in the first series of Probation Officer, 1959-62

Gabrielle Delal as Della Friedman, Hard Cases, 1988-89

The team from Hard Cases, 1988-89

Although a woman probation officer figured occasionally in later series of BBC cop show *Juliet Bravo*, it was 1988/89 before probation officers were again dramatised on TV, in two series of *Hard Cases*, set in and advised by Nottingham Probation Service. The characters and attitudes of the various team members, and the team politics, were convincing, but there was an excess of implausible action, and some too outlandish villains under supervision, though there were some touching ones too – the emotionally deprived rich kid, the burnt-out ageing armed robber. Ex-con turned actor Keith Allen swaggered as no-nonsense probation officer Jack Denby in the BBC serial *Jack of Hearts* (1999) even getting to assault a stroppy client in his office. Comedian Steve Coogan's breakthrough movie *The Parole Officer* (2001) missed every target and squandered his talent.

In *Cyclops* (2001), a one-off TV film, Juliey Aubrey played a probation officer of the near future, supervising a released sex offender by watching on her laptop everything that he sees, every place he goes, and everyone he meets through the miniature camera-tag implanted in his eye. When, one dark night, she sees the outside of her own house on screen she understandably starts worrying... but at least she stayed in the job. The probation officer protagonists in two American novels – Elmore Leonard's (1992) *Maximum Bob* and Peter Blauner's (1992) *Slow Motion Riot* both give up at the end, disillusioned, to retrain as cop and lawyer respectively.

Mike Nellis
Professor of Criminal and Community Justice
University of Strathclyde

Oral histories
Part 2

Gordon Read Exeter, Devon

Gordon Read worked in the Probation Service from 1962 to 1996. He was a probation officer for six years, during which time he was Secretary of his Napo Branch. He was a Senior in London and in Pentonville prison. He became an Assistant Principal Officer in Worcester and in 1981 Chief Officer for Devon.

On joining probation: 'I was in the army and remember people talking about becoming a probation officer. Then I went to university. I didn't give it much thought until, I suppose, my last year, when I started to think what am I now going to do? And I took myself off to Cambridge House in Bermondsey. The settlement, Cambridge House Settlement, and we did a week's introduction to social work in its widest sense. They took you round prisons and that's when I got interested.'

On a positive service: 'For me, I think the sense of a disciplined independence in using personal discretion. Essentially it was professionalism and not tick boxes. It was forming a judgement, expressing a view, but with a framework of understanding in which you placed the material you had, and then put forward a view about what was the most positive way of dealing with the person given all the circumstances. I never saw supervision indivisible from the assessment. It seemed to me that probation was about an integral approach to the person within the context of them being before the court, and trying to have some kind of integrity with which you approached the person faced with the possibility of losing their liberty to a greater or lesser degree. I think that's how I've always hoped that probation officers would be. When I talk to them now, I think they feel constrained, by OASys for example, which is bureaucratising something that could be much simpler in my view.'

On change: 'The thing that was most damaging to Probation was, I think, taking away the requirement of the defendant's agreement with the making of the Order, in both community service and probation. Because there's a hidden agreement given by prisoners when they are imprisoned, because you can't govern a prison without some kind of tacit consent of the prisoner. And I think, in the same way, it's an illusion that you can impose some kind of sanction through probation without the commitment of the participant. They're making it a punishment and the sentence of the court. Prior to that it was an Order of the court instead of a punishment. I think probation reflected the great strength of having an alternative to punishment in our society, because punishment is a dead end. This only satisfies a sort of mythical member of society and usually the people who are punished are the people who are punished day in day out, week in week out, year in year out, people who get the stick, people who got the birch, and they got it again and again. If you punish the people who shouldn't have punishment you create damage as well. The whole sense of the infliction of punishment is a negative concept, and that's why I think it was regrettable that the Act took away probation as an Order of the Court. They took away the duty of the court to seek the agreement of the person. There is an inherent weakness in getting involved with the punishment bit, because you don't change people by punishment. You entrench them or you humiliate them. '

On achievements: 'I think my main achievement was implementing a report commissioned by my predecessor for the provision of a partnership with police and the development of a protocol for the supervision of more dangerous offenders. It was established in 1982, probably 7 years before the Government really caught hold of it. We set up the notion of a Serious Offender Rehabilitation Team or SORT, as we called it. There was a team, and there was an arrangement whereby each of those involved in supervision had a plan that was as tight and informed as it could be. Not to put the person down or shackle them, but to be aware of what they were up to. In a sense the people who run the organisation needed to hold within themselves the emotional realities of doing the job. Holding the tension of trying to get alongside and motivate and get the cooperation of somebody who is potentially dangerous, and avoid becoming captured by them into ignoring the very real dangers.'

On national standards: 'I didn't welcome them. I didn't think they were strong enough. They were a face saving device really. A watch your back thing. They took away from the professional judgement of the staff. They were about the least you could do rather than the most you should be doing, and therefore they give the impression of something going on, which actually isn't and it discourages people from doing the job as they should do it according to the way they assess it.'

On management: 'I think the management was there to ensure that those with direct supervisory responsibility give as much of their time as was needed and reasonable to the people on the ground. Now I'm worried about, I suppose, an amoral, political administration, who thinks everything can be done by selling it off or seeing solutions entirely within business, rather than in public services. And that may be old fashioned, because I spring out of the 1948 revolution really. I mean that gave me chances as a child in terms of education, in terms of family, in terms of health, all those kind of things. And it created the really modern Probation Service – Schedule 5 of the '48 Act is very important and sometimes we don't go back to that enough. Because it abolished penal servitude and hard labour and corporal punishment as well as setting up the Service.'

Pam Bithell, Syd Matthew, Trisha Forsythe, Ann Russell, Diane Coombes, Gerald Perkins, Ben Grimsey

Devon and Cornwall Probation Service

Retired staff in Devon and Cornwall meet on a regular basis. Napo interviewed seven former members of staff in the summer of 2006.

On Probation

Pam Bithell: 'I've been in the Probation Service, based at Torquay, for 34 years. I'm not a probation officer like the rest of these people, I'm what was called the Court Administrative Officer, and I worked in the Service from 1967 to 1991.

Syd Matthews: 'I came to Devon in 1957. I beg your pardon, 1963. And I was here until 1988. In my 25 years I did a couple of years in

Gerald Perkins

Exeter, some in East Devon, back to Exeter and for the last thirteen and a half years I was Crown Court Liaison Probation Officer in Exeter Crown Court. I was a main grade probation officer throughout.'

Trisha Forsythe: 'I qualified in 1962 and worked in Manchester first, then Lancashire, became a Senior in Shropshire, and when my husband came down to Devon I came too and became a Senior, then a Social Worker, before coming back in 1982. I think I've had 40 different posts in Devon, before retiring in 1996.'

Ann Russell: 'I started as a mature entrant at Plymouth Poly in 1976. I then worked for 4 years for the Cornwall Probation Service before getting poached by Gordon Read who had tremendous problems filling his prisons. I was then seconded to Dartmoor and stayed there was a couple of years, and I then worked in Plymouth and Exeter as a Senior before retiring in 1999.

Diane Coombes: 'I started in Essex in September 1959 before moving to Devon three years later. I started in Newton Abbott, and at that stage women probation officers would always supervise women and boys up to 12. I later moved round the county before doing my last four years in Channings Wood and retired in May 1983. I was a main grade officer throughout that time.'

Gerald Perkins: 'I started off driving lorries and farming. I went to Southampton University and trained as a probation officer in 1969. The work was recommended to me by lads who'd worked with me and gone to prison. I worked in Berkshire before moving to Devon. I was an active member of the Probation Officers' Christian Union. I was always a standard officer, I never wanted to be a Senior at all.'

Ben Grimsey: 'I started up in Barnet and was there for four years. I also worked in Worcester. I came to Devon, and I stayed until 1988 when I retired. Before I'd been a teacher at a special school and did stints in two prisons. I actually had to pay £35 for the Education Officer to release me to train for Probation. I was in this wide area of community service and I liked that very much. I was so sick when they made it a punishment service. It was clear and it was firm but it was never punishment.'

On relationships

Gerald Perkins: 'Making people feel they were worthwhile. They are.'

Ann Russell: 'The personal relationships which one was able to have with clients, and then seeing them through everything - when you write their report, when you go to court with them and you supervise them.'

Ann Russell

Pat Bithell: 'And you cared about them'.

Diane Coombes: I actually also think that back in the days when all of us were starting out, in some respects it was much more of a national service then than it is now. I don't think we had national standards, I think there was a cross fertilisation that isn't as present as it used to be.'

Ann Russell: 'It was still very much a family, Probation. It was a rural community, and your team covered a huge area, but it was a community team.'

Syd Matthew: 'I used to get the reports, or give the reports, to my case committees and we used to meet once a month, and I found that very useful. Going back to the prisoners, I found that there was a very good relationship between the prisoners and the probation officers. Often in court I'd be called downstairs because a prisoner was creating trouble. I was the only one it seems, it sounds awfully big headed, to get the prisoners to see the sense before appearing before the magistrates.'

On respect

Syd Matthew: 'Judges, yes, often I appeared before them in fear and trepidation. We had good meetings with judges, they liked us.'

Ann Russell: 'We were very much officers of the court. We were protected by them to some extent. Certainly they rated probation as compared to social services in those days, social workers were seen as soft. We actually had status, which didn't matter in itself, but it didn't half open doors for you. We certainly used to have that status.

Trish Forsythe: 'We had more confidence. I mean the agencies were very different but I think we needed to appreciate that a lot of the way they were was because they hadn't got autonomy.'

Diane Coombes: 'The quality of reports that social workers did wasn't on a par, so I think it was a question of the fact that reports were our bread and butter. I also think that the main changes we've had since we were qualified had positive elements to them. I think it's sad now that we've thrown the baby out with the bath water. Some of the things that were happening in the service in our day were very exciting indeed.'

Trisha Forsythe

On positive initiatives

Ann Russell: 'I remember a thing called 'Starve the Borstals', when I was in Cornwall, spearheaded from the Home Office. We were obliged to meet as a community team to find ways of dealing with youngsters in the community and not sending them to the Borstal.'

Ben Grimsey: 'There was a youth support team that I headed up and that was the police, education, social services, and myself. We met, and every case referred by the police for going to court came to us and we decided who would be prosecuted. And the police every time took our advice. I was surprised how liberal the police were, well the ones that came on our group anyway.'

Diane Coombes: 'I actually think the service I joined was a vocation, and it became a very professional vocation. I actually think that to some degree now the service that exists is a job, or career perhaps, and is much more governed by procedures, which must be followed.'

Diane Coombes

Trisha Forsythe: 'But we were also, as probation officers, central to what was happening. Then quite rightly in one sense the task becomes centralised. There was a huge shake out and I assume that probation officers are not in the majority of probation staff as they were.'

Diane Coombes: 'Also when you went to the crown court you would be the probation officer for say Teignbridge petty session division. You were actually rooted. So it was my court, my committee, my area, and my clients. That was very positive and it felt like a vocation.'

Gerald Perkins: 'There was a sense of achievement from seeing people become strengthened. I remember one person I helped, who was very bright, who went to Dartmoor. I managed to get him into 'A' levels. I managed to sort of twist the Education Officer's arm for him to take studies and arrange to get him the books. And he went on and did very well for himself.'

On work experience

Ann Russell: 'It's amazing how much risk we used to handle before the days of risk management. Some of it was internalised because there weren't procedures for dealing with it, it just went with the territory. You handled risk. But it tended to work on the whole if you understand what I mean. I mean an amount of risk that was actually contained.'

Trisha Forsythe: 'When I first qualified, in the days when you took the little boys and girls and the women. I first worked in Manchester City and I was the only one who had a car. We used to hold report centres in church halls or whatever and perhaps not finish until 9 o'clock at night. My first caseload was 88. We worked terribly long hours.'

Pam Bithell

Pam Bithell: 'From a clerical angle, when I started in '67 we were in a derelict office down from the post office in Torquay. We were 3 floors up and we had 2 floors that were all falling down. In the mornings we used to have to go and pick-up the pigeon eggs, because they lived on our top floor. I worked for 5 officers on my own. We didn't have tape-recorders in those days. I did all this work, and I had two students, and everything was shorthand. I'd go through a complete shorthand book in 3 days, it was unbelievable how much work a clerical had to do in those days. At that time too we used to do all the adoption, and it was absolutely lovely when the children came in. Sometimes after they'd been adopted we had cakes and flowers and chocolates, and it was such a family orientated, loving, caring service.'

Ben Grimsey: 'We had in our team, when I first came in the first dozen years or so, caseloads of about 40. You could leave some, if you felt bold enough. You could say I'm leaving this order in abeyance. And I approved of that, in order to get on with the ones who needed work. You couldn't manage over 40 cases a week, so it was a decision you had to make.'

Syd Matthew: 'Only 40 cases! I can remember never having less than 80. When I took over the Crown Court, I insisted that I kept 40 on my caseload that I took with me to the Crown Court

Syd Matthew

so they didn't have to change from officer to officer. In court I often refused to read other peoples reports until I had made my relationship and done my own assessment, because I was not going to be prejudiced by the assessment of someone else.'

On security

Ben Grimsey: 'Security wasn't really an issue in those day. We had two waiting rooms and people would come in on aftercare from prison. We'd maybe have 20 in the waiting rooms, and how many times did we have trouble? We didn't have a lock on the door. They came in, wandered about, the secretaries spoke to them through the half open door. I think we only had one really dangerous situation with somebody in 20 years.'

Syd Matthew: 'No we did have more than that. The thing was my office used to be up on the 2nd floor. Then they moved me down and I was opposite where the clericals sat and where people came in. They had to take the flak, and to me that wasn't right. And I said if anyone gives you trouble give me a ring and I'll come out and sort it out. I think there must have been half a dozen serious ones in all the years I was there. I remember one man put a chair through the window.'

Gerald Perkins: 'Another one threw a mug through a window. He had a mug in his hand and threw it through the window.'

Diane Coombes: 'I once had a client who set the office on fire.'

Syd Matthew: 'Then we had a lady who was a bit difficult and wanted me to wash her down because she had got herself in such a state. And I said I'm not doing that and I gave her a bowl of water and a towel and insisted that she washed herself down. But it wasn't right for the clericals to have to put up with that.'

Ben Grimsey

On community service

Trisha Forsythe: 'One interesting anecdote is how the projects arose in community service. When community service started there were going to be 5 experiments, but Lord Cadbury, of the Cadbury Trust, was having dinner with the Home Secretary and asked him what was going on in criminal justice and learned about community service. He asked for the Cadbury Trust to be involved. So we had another pilot in Shropshire with the Cadbury Trust paying for a full time person to be based at the Iron bridge Museum and that person's job would be to find work within the area for community service offenders, and I was involved with setting that up.'

Ben Grimsey: 'The other positive thing about community service was when we had groups in village halls, church halls that sort of thing. It had a great impression on the community, because the people would come along very wary at first and then find it was just ordinary people, and their whole attitude changed to the groups. They were more sympathetic.'

Trisha Forsythe: 'The community service workers still to this day do some very impressive work.'

On joining and leaving

Pam Bithell: 'When I joined I'd already done 7 years with a big firm of solicitors in Torquay. I saw this advert for a secretary in the probation service. I thought that's is something I can do. I wanted to be in an organisation that was caring. When I joined I earned the princely sum of £12/10s/6p and I really did enjoy every minute I worked there until right near the end. It was the most wonderful experience and I've made some wonderful friends and I met my fiancé through it.'

Syd Matthew: 'There was nothing for kids, so I started cub scouts. I joined a local youth club and got involved with that sort of work. I thought I'd like to do this as a career. I applied to Nottingham University and did a course in youth and community work. When I left I thought the best thing I could do was work in Probation. I applied for a job and became a temporary probation officer.'

Trisha Forsythe: 'My father was a doctor and my mother was a full-time do-gooder. I did social services training and I did placements. I did one as an almoner but thought I couldn't carry on with that, so I shifted to generic training in social work. I was the third SPO in the Service. I was attracted to probation because I believed you could help people who were severely disadvantaged, particularly those who have ability, if only they re-channel their energies to do good rather than getting themselves into difficulties. I believe that to this day.'

Ann Russell: 'I left school with 5 'O' levels, became a shorthand typist, later got married and had my children, and swore I would never sit behind a typewriter again. I thought what can I do? They were advertising for probation officers in the press. I ended up with Home Office sponsorship. At that time I didn't want to work with children or with the elderly. I wanted to work with offenders. I went to Cornwall Probation and became a volunteer. I then became a probation officer and it's been a great, great career. I did feel effective. Well, you knew life well enough to know that your negatives in the services were going to outweigh your positives, but the positives kept me going. I felt effective. It almost felt like there was nowhere else for me to go'.

Diane Coombes: 'Many of us were members of the Devon Forum for Justice, we used to do restorative justice. It worked, we helped to retain offenders in the community. The biggest tragedy was taking away 'advise, assist and befriend'.

Ken Ward Teignmouth, Devon

Ken Ward worked in the Probation Service from 1963 to 1996. He was assistant warden in a Probation Hostel in Sheffield. He worked in Wakefield and Exeter prisons where he became a Senior and then worked in several community teams in Devon. He was a Napo NEC Rep for a number of years and was also branch chair.

On joining probation: 'I'd been a fitter for five years, and loved it. I did National Service and I liked that as well. I was in the military police. I came out and served two years as a toolmaker. I then saw this job in Sheffield and thought I'll go for this, and I took to it like a duck to water – working with young kids. They were a super bunch of lads.'

On positive experiences: 'Everything, everything was positive. It used to drive my family nuts, I'm not joking. For years on end, until I retired, I used to go off to work whistling and come back whistling. It wasn't a job was it really? They gave you some money to go out and enjoy yourself. It was terrific stuff – interfering with peoples' lives. You never had anybody nasty. A few lifers in Wakefield Prison. A few that you'd never let out again. But it was terrific stuff. I think that generic system helped to level the difficulties that people had really, dealing with very young people, dealing with divorce courts, dealing with crown courts.'

On caseloads: 'I think individuals were able to manage very large caseloads of very diverse characters but not a lot of squealing about stress. There was obviously, stress but people didn't talk about it too much. I'd start with 80 cases but it could go up to 100.'

On cases: 'I remember one case, a man I was supervising in the mid-'80s. He was in a council house and he'd been left with seven children. His wife had left. Only one of them was working. Needless to say he was being done for DSS fraud. But this man did a lot, he did all the housework, cooking, cleaning, ironing, gardening – he did all of it on his own. If he had spare time he decorated for some people at £1 an hour. He kept records of everything and he was being hauled up before the court. When I found out what he was getting I phoned DSS and said is this right? They discovered they hadn't been paying him what they should have been paying for years. I said I would make sure this was mentioned in the report, the magistrates must know about it. I refused to cover it up. He went to court and everyone was expecting this scrounger to get three years. When everything was explained he got two years probation and of course he then got his benefits. I felt he was a really good man. He was the salt of the earth.'

On making a difference: 'I would say that at times of emotional or marital stress we managed to make things a little easier from time to time, particularly with young offenders. Let them appreciate that they are no different to the rest of us but they'd come across circumstances they couldn't cope with. The little lad who lost his dad suddenly in a car accident. The lad who lost his mother and we found him sleeping in a chicken run because he was wetting the bed. He said that was the best place for him. I do believe from experience that your prolific offenders often become your serious offenders. They start initially offending at the age of 14 and when they get to 25 you worry that the next burglary might be the one they use a knife or a brick on someone's head. I think when you look at resources given to look after serious offenders they mustn't be mixed up with people who are supervising ordinary cases. You just can't do it.'

On the future: 'I don't know about the future but I do know we need direction from people who are fairly confident about what they are talking about, based on research. The stuff I read in probation papers, some of it from criminologists, some of it does not fill me with hope. People are kite flying. I'm not sure what the purpose of end to end offender management is but I'm not sure that it will ever work. I'm not sure it can because every prison governor has his own agenda. He knows how many staff he's got, how many activities he has and beyond that there's not really anything. We don't want criminologists going flying off at tangents, we want a service that is properly managed, not a service that gets kicked right, left and centre. The press just love it.'

Joyce Belcher, Vernon Young, Jack Mayhew, Keith Watson

Joyce Belcher was appointed a probation officer from 1 April 1950 and worked with the Service until September 1985. She was a main grade officer throughout her career and was also membership secretary for Napo in Surrey.

Vernon Young joined the Probation Service in September 1967 and retired in December 1999. He was a main grade and Senior probation officer in Surrey and Hampshire. He was branch chair for Napo until his retirement.

Jack Mayhew, joined the Probation Service in 1960 after completing a Home Office course. He worked first in Woking Surrey and then moved to Farnham where he stayed until 1981 when he retired, but continued to work part-time until 1995, into his late 70s.

Keith Watson, joined the Probation Service in 1960 as a direct entrant in Inner London. He worked there until 1987 when he retired.

On joining Probation

Jack Mayhew: When I was a Boys Brigade Officer and had a company in South London I was asked by solicitors to speak for one of the lads who was at court. I was there all day, and at lunchtime they said they didn't need me. I'd seen quite a lot of what was going on and I thought these young lads I've got in the Boys Brigade generally don't get into trouble but there were many I saw in court that day that I thought perhaps I ought to spend more time with them. So at that moment I decided I'd meet the probation officer. I thought this is what I'd like to do. I'd like to do something more positive, something that helped young people in trouble. That's why I decided to become a probation officer. When I got in there was such a variety of duties. It seemed a great avenue of opportunity to do things that I'd never even considered before. I think this was a challenge to me.'

Vernon Young: 'I joined as a mature student and went through the Home Office course, which was very, very good. I joined because I cared and because everybody kept telling me I was a good listener. And I always thought that listening was very important in dealing with people. The highlight of my career was the ability to remain with people through all the problems that they had, and not give up on them, and be honest and straight with them. Another highlight of my career was the court welfare service and the mediation work that we started and then spread throughout the country, enabling us to do in-court mediation. I also conducted over a thousand interviews with parents getting them to talk about what was in the best interests of their children. It happened to be something that suited me, and thankfully the vast majority never came to court again.'

Joyce Belcher

Joyce Belcher: 'I was in the WAAF during the war. Towards the end colleagues were talking about what we were going to do when we were demobbed, what training we were going to have. I decided to go to Southampton and do a 2 year social studies certificate. First I worked in psychiatric social work, then at a youth club. I also worked as a Moral Welfare Worker dealing with unmarried mothers. And then one term I worked with a probation officer in Farnham and I decided that was the thing

I wanted to specialise in. I applied to the Home Office, got on their course and then worked in Hampshire on a placement. I found I liked working with families and individuals in trouble, it kept me going, and now I could never imagine doing anything else.'

Keith Watson: 'I started off in local government as a youth employment officer. Then a friend of mine who had applied to join the Probation Service came back full of enthusiasm and showed me some of the stuff he was doing. That kindled my interest in the Probation Service, I thought it could be an outlet for me. I saw an advert in the papers and shot off an application. I found it was for me. I didn't come from an academic background but an industrial background, and this was really what I wanted. We used to sit and debate things it was fantastic. It wasn't just mundane stuff. Often it was esoteric stuff that might change the world. It was extraordinary, it was positive.'

On initiatives

Jack Mayhew: 'I came out of the Rainer House training course in Chelsea, which was quite an education in some ways, and I was appointed to Woking as a main grade officer. I later moved to Farnham where I stayed until 81 when I retired. I remember working with a Travellers camp in Ash. I remember the work well. We had an alternative to custody unit at Woking, that met on 2 nights a week.'

Keith Watson: 'We had problems with the the juvenile centre at Send. All the kids had to be farmed out to other prisons. The prisoners had gone mad. They wanted someone to go in and sort them out. There was myself, another male and 3 female officers. We found a riot squad out with dogs; the fire service was there ready to hose people down; prison officers sitting on the chests of prisoners; glass was smashed everywhere. The way we decided to proceed was to make sure everybody got a phone call, to tell their wives, families where they were and not to visit for a while, at least for a few days. So we had to flog through this, working 12 hours a day, two weekends, to make sure we got parole records reasonably straight, as straight as we could, and that everybody knew where everybody was. It was quite exciting but it was tiring, but we got through the work.'

Jack Mayhew

Joyce Belcher: 'One of my colleagues in Farnham noticed that when people came to report, in the waiting room they talked to each other and learned all sort of things. When they came into the office they clammed up and didn't really discuss much. So we started this alternative probation project where they could come on a daily basis as a requirement of a probation order and get involved in activities and socialising, learn how to use a telephone, how to fill in a form, that sort of thing. But it led to much deeper things, all sort of discussions and outings to places. It ran for a number of years. It was really exciting and led to the setting up of a detoxification centre and later the Surrey Community Development Trust.'

On supervising clients

Joyce Belcher: 'When I was first appointed it was in West Cumberland where I had 6 courts. I stayed there for a couple of years before moving to Surrey and later worked in Greater London. In those days women officers supervised girls, females and little boys only. After boys became 12 they had to go to the male officers. We did matrimonial work. We did through-care work. We dealt with neighbours quarrels. We had to mediate between neighbours who had quarrels. If it came to court sometimes it was referred to us. We weren't actually responsible for placing children for adoption but we did the Guardian Ad Litem work and also divorce court welfare'.

Keith Watson: 'It was 1st January 1968. That's when men were first allowed to supervise women. That's when parole was introduced as well. It was a very important date that, it changed a lot. Men were then allowed to supervise girls and woman. They weren't allowed to do that before because of all the inferences.'

Vernon Young: 'I remember the introduction of men being able to supervise women for the first time. I liked this idea. I always felt that women were more likely to open up to men. Although I do remember once breaching a woman and her mother stood up and said why was she being supervised by a male officer, and the court ordered the case be transferred to a female colleague. I stormed up to the magistrate and complained. I was very angry but was obviously wrong to have an outburst in court.'

Vernon Young

On achievements

Keith Watson: 'I think the business about cohesion is the one for me. I really thought that what we were doing, what my colleagues were doing, was working for the good of the community and the individual. We went to fantastic national conferences.'

Vernon Young: 'I think we achieved a lot as a court welfare service. You had an opportunity to put parents together to consult about the best interests of the children. The court ordered it, so you had an automatic 'in' to a situation where there was no cooperation. I think it was a really positive achievement.'

Joyce Belcher: 'It was great setting up prisoners' wives groups. They did a lot of good work. We used voluntary associates. They gave a lot of help in getting prisoners to resettle.'

On cases

Keith Watson

Keith Watson: 'I remember Jimmy. He'd come down from the North East and got himself in trouble. He turned up wearing a leather hat, dark glasses, looking very threatening. Nobody could understand him because of his broad Geordie accent. I took the case on. I remember he never changed his socks. Never, ever changed them. He'd never shake hands. Constantly getting in and out of trouble. He got arrested, hit the police man. He would always end up at our Probation office. In and out of hospital suffering from stress. He used to write poetry. We kept working with him. The sad thing was though he died at 35 of cancer. He found out once where the Chief Officer lived and went round to his house. The police had to go and find him. It was so sad that he died when there was so much potential.'

Joyce Belcher: 'I remember once I had to supervise a man going to a family funeral who'd been charged with incest. Within the family there had been a reconciliation and his mother died and he was allowed a day's leave from prison to go to the funeral. I sat discreetly at the back. It could have been embarrassing. Later I remember he was refused parole and I had to go round to the house and tell them that that's what had happened. The whole family cried. I went in the house and sat down with them, calmed them down, told them eventually he would get parole and be allowed home.'

The future

Keith Watson: 'I'm really hurt at the amount of criticism that's been chucked at the Probation Service over the last months. Quite unbelievable! I don't know the Probation Service anymore. I don't understand the acronyms - a different language is being spoken. The business of setting targets, what on earth are these targets? It's like a foreign language.'

Vernon Young: 'I'm the most recently retired of the Hampshire group and I have noticed tremendous change. Everything's geared to paperwork. I know people didn't used to worry enough, but now there's so much emphasis on paperwork and accountability. Not accountability to the client but accountability to the Home Office. It seems to me that it's just moving more and more in that direction and getting away from the things that we came into probation for in the first place. It's all very worrying. It seems to be that the probation officer is held accountable for what they are supposed to do not held accountable for actual work with the clients.'

Michael Day and Basil Hylton Ludlow, Shropshire

Michael Day was appointed as a probation officer in 1960, as a Principal Probation Officer in 1968, and as Chief Probation Officer for the West Midlands from 1976 to 1988, when he left to become Chief Executive of the Commission for Racial Equality. He was Chairman of the Conference of Chief Probation Officers from 1973 to 1976.

Basil Hylton commenced training in October 1970 at Bristol. He worked as a probation officer in Gloucestershire, was appointed a Senior Probation Officer in the West Midlands in 1978 and was Assistant Chief from 1985 until he retired in 1996.

On Courts and files

Michael Day: 'Things have changed amazingly. At the beginning we had case committees and all the case committee material went to the magistrates. We actually handed over our files and they looked at them.'

Basil Hylton: 'Yes, I'd go and see a member of the Magistrates' Committee, and although by that time we were hesitating to hand over files we were expected to discuss cases.'

Michael Day: 'It was an appalling ritual. You used to meet, I don't know, every two months. You'd stand outside in a corridor and each was called in turn to present their cases to this group of magistrates. You used to wait there for hours. It was then a period of uncomfortable transition and you can imagine there was a lot of resistance. You were taking influence and authority away from the bench, particularly over their probation officers. I remember when I was first Chief I was confronted with my committee which was something like 68 people. It was so big they couldn't sit round a table. My struggle as Chief was to reduce that number of magistrates to about 20. It was a real battle.'

On joining

Basil Hylton: 'I came from Jamaica actually to study for the priesthood. The first thing that I became aware of was that I wanted to become involved in helping the poor and in issues around poverty and oppression. What I was being trained for wasn't going to lead me to that so I terminated my studies. I thought I'd go back to Jamaica. That ended with Enoch Powell's announcement on

Basil Hylton

"rivers of blood". I was encouraged by my brother who was living in London to stay a bit longer and do some work. I wrote to the Home Office and said if I apply for training how long would you require me to work here? They said 3 years. Of course 3 became 6, 6 became 10 and now its 40 next year. In the end I trained and applied to be a probation officer. I was taken aback in my first interview when I was asked how I felt the white community would accept me. For a start I couldn't understand where the question was coming from. Secondly, during my entire training the people I actually worked with were white and there was an underlying assumption that somehow I might not be up to the work. And in many ways that question pinpointed a number of important things.'

'Since the beginning as a probation officer I'd often go to clients doors. I'd written I was coming, but when they saw me they wouldn't let me in the house. On one occasion I was standing at a door and told the woman if I wasn't allowed in I would not be able to write a report and her son would stay in Borstal. She let me in and invited me to sit down. I refused to sit, demanding an apology first. It took a bit more time but the apology was eventually forthcoming.

'I soon found I had no real support as a black officer. I created my own support from outside the Probation Service. I identified a couple of black nurses, a black teacher, a black magistrate. We had a group of about nine of us who met each month outside the Probation setting to exchange our experiences and support each other.'

On Black Probation Officers

Michael Day: 'With very strong reservations I remember in the West Midlands, we supported the idea of a Association of Black Probation Officers, and there was a Committee issue – magistrates committee issue – as to whether we should allow them time, as it were in working hours, to attend meetings and whether they would be paid expenses for travelling to meetings in London. It was by no means an easy argument to win. The Treasurer of the Committee in particular resisted it on the grounds that they weren't an authorised body.'

Basil Hylton: 'That's right. We approached you Michael, as Head of ACOP for support, but there was no doubt about the support that Michael gave us. In fact this was actually quite important because when I speak to the Police Federation for example I sing the praise of Napo because it was Napo who stood out and supported the formation of the Association even before ACOP did, and in the end Napo said it would pay the travelling expenses and the only criteria was that people had to be bona fide members, which seemed fair enough.'

Michael Day: 'I remember discussions we had at that time and Basil must take credit for shifting the mood. I remember you saying without such a grouping there could be no combined articulation of the black perspective. I'm sure this was the kind of argument that persuaded the Home Office and Committees that you needed black staff to draw strength from meeting together. Indeed I think it is one of the great tragedies of the Metropolitan Police that for years those arguments weren't accepted.'

Basil Hylton: 'I remember the Monday following the riots in Handsworth when we all went down to meet Douglas Hurd. We were walking down a back street and about a dozen black men looking fairly rough were walking up the street. We decided we'd go on and as we walked away one of the men came up and grabbed me and said "who is this, what are you doing here dressed up" and one of the Rastafarians shouted "leave him alone, he's a probation officer, I know him". He said, oh right and off he went. And that's part of what I'm saying about being part of the community and known to the community. And that wasn't just about being black because Michael might have other views about this particular person and that community.'

Michael Day: 'But you had to be very good at your job, Basil, to hold it down, because if you'd failed it would have set the whole process back a long time, just like the first woman Chief Probation officer they appointed in Sheffield in about 1945. She struggled and it took another 20 years before they appointed another woman.'

On reflections

Michael Day: 'All the projects we were involved in were long term. The investment and the effort that we put into the community was a 5 to 10 year plan. We're now in the business of much quicker fixes and the investment will not be made in aspects of the Probation Service unless they can show quick results. We couldn't demonstrate that it would reduce the offending behaviour within the next 2 or 3 years in Handsworth, but it did because people worked imaginatively. It wasn't just about imposing authority and law and order, it was about engaging with people in a kind of struggle. And the sadness is that not enough money went into it. It wasn't across the board, it was a deprived area in terms of services: schools, and health and welfare. You can't correct that now. It's really sad that probation has moved away from the community.'

Basil Hylton: 'Exactly. Just before I left in 96 I actually did a sampling of 300 reports from my officers because I wanted to prove a point. Something like 78 per cent were done without home visits. How can you say that you're actually presenting knowledge and information if you don't go to see them in their home, where they can entertain you in their domain. I know we're in a position through health & safety that people feel they might be attacked and so on, but what's happened is we've alienated ourselves from the kind of people we would in the past have been very close to. The issue about advise, assist and befriend was crucial to your attitude and engagement with the offender.'

On professionalism

Michael Day: 'We were very patronised – maybe we're still patronised – in the past. On the whole probation officers were seen as a bit below the salt. To claim any kind of professionalism when compared to the lawyers and the clerks of the court was being a bit presumptuous. So I think that I and the other group of people who were with me who were all graduates were able to establish that we weren't stupid. That not only did we know which knife and fork to use but that you could present a professional argument on issues to do with the criminal justice system and individuals and society and that was important at that time.'

Michael Day

Michael Day: 'I think alongside professionalism I would put providing a real service. I think there was a strong sense, and I'm not saying it isn't there now, but people saw themselves as providing a real service to the community of which they were a part. And it was long term. Many Seniors were there for many years. They were part of the team, part of the community, they felt it and they knew it.'

On achievements

Basil: 'Besides working with groups of offenders the other thing was to see the development of officers working in a team. Team work is essentially about ensuring that people supplement or complement each others practice, drawing on different people's strength for the benefit of the clients. I mean I've seen this happen. I've worked with it, part of my job has been to enable it. The most satisfying part of my own practice was about forging relationships with clients and offenders on the basis that they attend for certain kinds of treatment. I guess now they would turn up for some to tick a box. Turn up you get a tick.'

Michael: I feel strongly about where the service has gone wrong. I had a tremendous battle within ACOP in the last 3 years when I was in the service because I saw it being sold out by certain managers, in a kind of knee jerk reaction to politicians. It is not clear, unlike the kind of work we've described to you already, in which the leadership was thinking about where the service wants to go. There seems to be no one at the moment thinking about the service and where it wants to go. The Probation Service has never gone down the road of seeking to consult the community, and that would have offered in my view a kind of leadership much more in line with what I experienced earlier in my career. What we've done is hand the management of the service over to the politicians rather than maintaining it in the hands of the professionals.

The history of LAGIP

The Staff Support Group for Lesbians, gay men, bisexuals and transgendered staff working in Probation and Family Courts.

During the 1970s the Gay Rights movement developed. More militant than its reformist predecessors it took to the streets and demanded equal rights. It was part of a greater movement. Women and Black People had shifted to this more assertive position. It was part of the demand for more personal freedom that surfaced in the 1960s.

At the AGM in 1976 at Harrogate a group of lesbian and gay Napo members got together spontaneously because they were tired of the level of heterosexism and homophobia being expressed both at the Conference and in the workplace.

At that AGM two gay men succeeded in a motion which committed Napo to support the campaign for the equalisation of the age of consent and getting Napo to affiliate to CHE. The campaign succeeded after more than twenty years!

In 1982 this informal group formed LAGIP and was formally recognised as an autonomous group by Napo the following year, With the aid of sympathetic heterosexual colleagues Napo was persuaded to include lgbt issues in all its equal rights policies and also on professional issues. Napo with Unison led the move to ensure the TUC also took on our campaigns, leading to the formation of the LGBT TUC Conference. Napo had taken up the cause long before most unions.

Napo has for many years given an annual grant to LAGIP, which until recently was its only source of income.

LAGIP's main role was to provide support and an opportunity for lgbt staff to get together and gain strength and confidence. This was especially important for those who felt isolated and those who were subjected to bigotry and persecution.

The 1990s was a period of change. There was the Aids scare and the Tory Government's antipathy to 'homosexuality' leading to Clause 28, forbidding the teaching of homosexuality in schools in any positive fashion. It felt at one point as if all the gains of the previous twenty years might be lost. However, the decision of the lgbt community to fight back gave the campaign a boost. The European Directive, which in turn led to the reforms that followed the change of Government in 1997.

The Labour Government was often tentative, relying on free votes in Parliament rather than Government Policy.

As we entered the new millennium LAGIP realised it also had to change. At its bi annual Conference held in Norwich in 2000 a decision was made to review our structure and who qualified for membership. A Steering Committee was formed and it recommended that membership should include bisexuals and transgendered staff. Although the issues can be different for lesbians, gay men, bisexuals and transgendered people the oppression they experience has a common root.

It was also felt that LAGIP needed a more formal structure with its leadership accountable to members and communicating more effectively with the Probation Service.

LAGIP entered into negotiations with the National Probation Directorate and by 2002 was formally recognised as the Staff Support Group for lgbt people in the Probation Service. As an Autonomous Group of Napo it continued to include people working in CAFCASS but still needs to set up a system that supplies the same level of support.

The NPD agreed to fund LAGIP. The level of funding is an ongoing issue and is not sufficient. This has meant LAGIP has had to focus on staff issues despite its wish to also include service delivery issues and support for lgbt service users.

LAGIP has progressed from being a small protest movement to an organisation recognised and respected by employers and senor managers.

Its membership has doubled in the last three years. It also offers honorary membership to none lgbt people who are willing to support the cause.

Recent changes in legislation has made it more important for the Service to change along the lines that LAGIP has been urging for many years. These include the Gender Recognition Act, The Employment Directive on Sexual Orientation in the Workplace and hopefully an amended Equality Act will include goods and services.

LAGIP and Napo need to do more work on bisexual and transgender issues as well as continue to demand equality for lesbians and gay men. The fact that it took LAGIP a long time to persuade those in authority to remove 'homosexuality' as a factor in OGRES to access risk of reoffending is evidence that there is a lot more to be done.

Michael Lloyd
Convenor, and later Chair, of
LAGIP from 1998-2005

The history of ABPO

During the 1950s and 60s Bristol was by no means unique in how it treated its Caribbean immigrants. As a former slave trading port it could have been more amenable to their presence. Thus, a newly arrived black student might be forgiven for thinking that names such as Clifton's 'Blackboy Hill' and 'Whiteladies Road' were signifying a familiarity with black people on those very streets. Alas, our observant student would soon note the absence of live black faces. Such was the context in which ABPO was first conceived: looking into a mirror that reflects a mere shadow of oneself.

Yet, in St Pauls, Bristol, black people were far from invisible or silent. In 1963 Bristol experienced a bus boycott whose publicity divided opinions in the city, capturing world-wide attention. Harold Wilson, Tony Benn, and Sir Laurie Constantine all figured in this local story that helped to raise the nation's consciousness about racial injustice in the UK. The result? The employment of a few black bus conductors and drivers, the illegalising of racial discrimination at work some

five years later, and St Pauls remained the 'black area'. Race was always about keeping people apart, and the more imperceptibly the better.

If getting bus conductors' jobs was novel, becoming a probation officer was perhaps a more challenging proposition. For a start, the more favoured route of entry was via military or established churches' backgrounds. These structured exclusion of black people from most statutory public services sent clear 'don't-come not-wanted' messages to black communities. Indeed, notwithstanding the goodwill of many, the fact was that black commonwealth British subjects were at the very least treated as if they had no legal or moral right to be there.

Aware that authentic self-empowerment was not going to be given (but taken), we soon learnt that professionally isolated black social workers, teachers, supervisory nurses, and even the then sole black magistrate of Bristol were themselves also facing this daily hurdle of racial rejection. Thus, we came together under a common umbrella group, the Bristol Black

Social Workers Association, to offer ourselves mutual and appropriate support. In doing so we also formed a bridge between our distinctly alienated communities and our respective services by setting up out of working hours community advice 'surgeries'.

By the late 1970s an increasing number of black POs were coming on stream, particularly in the West Midlands. To us, meeting as black (and Asian) probation staff felt right, and my experience of Bristol added to our confidence. Our major concerns related to the disproportionate level of incarceration of the black community, and thereby with 'racism within the service'. These were voiced through Napo, distracting it from its then 'leftist' preoccupations about the National Front. By 1981 the majority of West Midlands black officers formed the nucleus of ABPO, still meeting outside working hours and at members own expense. Knowledge of these meetings generated some personal animosity in many white staff who felt that they were being betrayed and viewed by us as 'racists'. The early support of the CPO, (Sir) Michael Day, was instrumental in gradually securing support from ACOP.

ABPO's dual aim had always been to ensure ongoing support to black staff and to holding service management and union to account in relation to experiences of black staff. The reality of institutional racism was known and experienced by ABPO long before the Stephen Lawrence Inquiry affirmed its existence.

However, from its outset ABPO had made it clear that it was not trying to pursue sectional interests of black minority ethnic staff; but seeking professional changes and a type of governance that would enable the full contribution by black staff in and through anti-racist professional support and practice. It was never meant to represent or pursue the exclusive interests of specific staff groups. Others have since taken a different view.

Neither should the crucial support of ABPO by Napo be underestimated. Napo has always focused on the greater hope that ABPO members would in time seek fuller active participation within Napo. In 2006 black staff within the NPS, though still seeking to ensure anti-racist professional support and practice, seem more of themselves – and less of shadows.

Basil W. Hylton
Co-Founder and first
chair of ABPO
ACPO West Midlands,
1985-96

History of the Edridge Fund

Sydney Edridge, who was the first Chair of Napo in 1907, had always been a great admirer and supporter of the Probation Service as well as a real friend, so that when he died in 1934 the National Executive decided to set up a benevolent fund, the aim of which was to 'alleviate cases of distress amongst retired officers and to assist serving officers in need of urgent help'. It was a very fitting tribute and memorial that the fund should be known as the Edridge Benevolent Fund. At that time the fund was financed by contributions from serving officers and others interested in probation.

In 1945 the annual conference of Napo instituted the Constitution and Rules which require the NEC to maintain a fund known as the Edridge Benevolent Fund. The hope was that all probation officers would pay five shillings per year into the fund to support those in need. Although funding was less than hoped, the fund has been maintained.

In 1969 there was a possibility that Napo might join forces with BASW and it was decided that the funds of Edridge should be wholly administered as a charitable trust so that it would be a separate independent charity.

In the early years of the fund grants made were largely to retired police court missionaries and probation staff who had not benefited from pensions. Gradually, particularly with the influx of student Probation Officers, funds have been expended on serving staff.

Present day

Today, the eligibility to benefit from the Edridge Fund has widened to cover all those who are eligible to be members of Napo, and their dependants. The lifeblood of Edridge funding is sustained because Napo has agreed to donate between one and two percent of its subscription income to Edridge, which gives the fund some 40 percent of its income. Other funds raised include interest on investments and fundraising throughout the country by individuals and groups.

At present the fund remains administered similarly to seventy years ago. There are five Trustees, each appointed by the NEC and serving a period of five years. There is a small part-time secretariat administering the fund. At present the number of applications during a year is around 120, and the breakdown amongst grades is as follows:
2 SPOs, 32 POs, 9 Retired POs, 22 PSOs, 1 Retired PSO, 25 1st year TPOs, 28 2nd year TPOs, and 1 other grade.

Each branch elects an Edridge Representative, who support applicants and help with fundraising and public relations. They can be of immense help to those in need.

Type of help provided

Reasons for applications have varied between bankruptcy, mental health issues leading to long-term sickness, and a relationship breakdown resulting in financial distress.

One of the many letters of thanks stated 'There is no doubt that without your assistance the next month would have been very bleak. You can be assured that the grant you sent will be paying for living, travel and study costs in the coming weeks.'

Richard Martin
Edridge Secretary

Centenary Congratulations

Brendan Barber, General Secretary, TUC

The Probation Service is one of the UK's most vital public services, and it is high time we recognised the huge contribution it makes to our national life. For one hundred years, the service has helped damaged and vulnerable people rehabilitate themselves and rebuild their lives, while reducing reoffending and protecting society. Today – despite huge pressures on staff – the Probation Service is performing at consistently high levels, with just 0.6 per cent of high-risk offenders committing further serious offences. But the government's plans to introduce contestability into the service threatens to undermine these achievements. We must protect the unique public service ethos that lies at the heart of the Probation Service.

Brendan Barber

Cindy Barnett, Chairman, Magistrates' Association

The magistrates' courts rely very heavily on the advice and support given to them by the Probation Service. Sentencing is a complex and difficult matter; magistrates have a wide menu of options under the Criminal Justice Act 2003 and it is of great help to have professional advice as an aid to their sentencing decision. It is also immensely important that courts should have confidence in those enforcing the community penalties that they have imposed. The probation service has gone through many changes and the pace of change seems to increase without pause, but in providing an increasing range of approved programmes probation staff have built up skills, experience, expertise and qualifications to provide a professional and effective service to offenders, the courts and the community.

MAGISTRATES
ASSOCIATION
▲

Rt Hon Alan Beith MP, Liberal Democrat

The Probation Service, dating back to the original 'Police Court missionaries', has an honourable and distinguished history of taking on one of society's most difficult jobs, securing the rehabilitation of offenders. Remarkable people have done this work with great courage, patience and skill. Yet in the last decade members of the service have been endlessly drawn into plans for reorganisation, and redirection, while sections of the press and some politicians have undervalued and undermined their work. Society needs to recognise much more clearly the importance, the value and the tough challenges posed by working with offenders.

Alan Beith

The Rt Hon Hilary Benn MP, Labour, former Probation Minister 2002-03

During my time as a Minister for Prisons and Probation, I was fortunate to meet a group of professional, dedicated individuals who were working hard both to protect the public and to try and help individuals to move away from a life that was damaging both themselves and others. I was very aware that the public knew very little about the work of the Probation Service and that if they knew more they, too, would be impressed by the efforts being made to protect them. In particular, I was really impressed by the efforts made to develop the multi agency public protection arrangements which deal with serious and sexual offenders; these showed just what could be done when all the agencies concerned came together to pool their knowledge and resources. It's challenging and demanding work being a Probation officer, but I know that there are many individuals whose lives have been helped by the efforts of the probation Service and in this Centenary Year we should pause to say thanks as we face up to the challenges that lie ahead.

Lord Carlile of Berriew QC

The Probation Service has an honourable history. If we are to remain a civilised and just society, constructive alternatives to imprisonment for crime are of paramount importance. The Probation Service has the highest expertise in this work. The future needs every bit of that skill.

Tony Benn, writer, broadcaster and campaigner

I have always regarded the Probation Service as an independent, principled and positive part of our legal system with a unique role in helping us to make sense of the arguments about crime and the rehabilitation of offenders at a moment when the tabloids seem to have been allowed to dictate policy.

Sir Ian Blair, Commissioner of the Metropolitan Police

The Metropolitan Police has a history of close working with the Probation Service, which over recent years has seen strong partnerships at local level within CDRPs and Borough Criminal Justice Groups in London and at strategic level in the London Criminal Justice Board. The work we jointly do ranges from the management of Prolific and Priority Offenders, who are responsible for large amounts of crime and criminal activity, to protecting the public from high risk individuals through MAPPA.

This work has been a contributory factor in the continuing success in driving down crime in London and in our enhanced capability to protect the public.

I congratulate the Probation Service on its centenary and look forward with confidence to building on our strong relationship in the future, in the interests of making London safer for those who live, work and visit here.

METROPOLITAN POLICE

Nick Clegg MP, Liberal Democrat Shadow Home Secretary

Few public services can be as readily overlooked as the probation service. For the last century probation officers have tirelessly and selflessly sought to help make our society safer and to rehabilitate those who have been drawn towards crime. The role they play is a vital one and it is important that politicians from across the party spectrum recognise this. As the second century of the probation service begins it is crucial that the unglamorous, painstaking, yet hugely important work of the probation service is cherished, not undermined, by both Government and opposition parties.

Lord Dholakia, Deputy Leader, Liberal Democrats

The National Probation Service has played a major role in reducing crime and assisting offenders in the process of rehabilitation. Probation officers provide a valuable service to our courts in reaching decisions about sentencing. The twin aims of protecting the public and diverting offenders away from crime and criminality have been at the forefront of probation officers' roles. We can all take pride in the way they have carried out their duties.

Geoff Dobson, Deputy Director, Prison Reform Trust

At its heart Probation has always been about dedicated professionals working with offenders to help them find a legitimate sense of purpose and develop the internal controls to enable them to pursue it. This painstaking, demanding work by 'caring authority figures' has drawn where possible on family and community resources. The Centenary is an opportunity to look back with pride and to shape the future with renewed strength and confidence.

David Faulkner, former Deputy Permanent Secretary, Home Office

In my time in the Home Office I hoped I could help the probation service (still without capital letters) to become more influential and more effective, not only in expanding the use of community penalties but also in using its skills, experience and inspiration to promote what would now be called criminal justice reform. It would become part of a more inter-connected criminal justice system, more closely integrated into its local communities. Liberal values and with them the probation service later lost much of the respect they once enjoyed, and the present government's vision of the National Probation Service is as an agency of public protection and an arm of government. But I would not care for a society, or a criminal justice system, from which liberal ideas were absent or the Service's traditions were lost.

Edward Garnier QC MP, Shadow Minister for Home Affairs and Conservative Spokesman on the Probation Service

The Probation Service has played, and continues to play, an invaluable part in the delivery of justice for the last century. Through its role in public protection, reducing re-offending, and rehabilitating offenders, it is vital for the proper working of the criminal justice system. Since 1907 when offender supervision was put on a statutory basis, the valuable and valued work of the Probation Service has been recognised by judges, parliamentarians and public policy-makers – and by offenders and their victims. But no public service can stand still and the Probation Service will adapt to the changing circumstances within which it has to operate. Some changes will be organic and the result of new thinking from the staff of the Service; some, as in the last few years, will be sudden, ill-considered and unhelpful. We are about to enter another period of change and upheaval so this centenary falls at a crucial time in the history of the Service. It is vital that we advance carefully and thoughtfully to ensure that any new demands respect the requirements of justice and public protection as opposed to those of the short term and political expedience. A Conservative government would not rule out private or not-for-profit provision of probation functions alongside the Probation Service so long as it meets the needs of local communities, those under supervision, and the high standards of professionalism in public protection that the public has seen from the Probation Service. There is no doubt that crime will still be with us over the next 100 years so it is imperative that we ensure that the Probation Service, its ethos and its professionalism remain with us too as we work to provide both safety and security for the people of this country.

Cheryl Gillan MP, Conservative, Shadow Minister for Wales

From 1907 to 2007 the Probation Service has played a crucial role in the criminal justice system. Since 1907, when offender supervision was put on a statutory basis, the admirable work of the service has been recognized by judges, parliamentarians and Ministers as well as by victims of crime and offenders.

The Probation Service is currently facing great changes which will be imposed through legislation. Any new demands on it must respect the requirements of justice and public protection as opposed to those of the short term and political expedience. If not for profit or private provision of probation is envisaged it must function alongside the Probation Service on the strict understanding that the needs of local communities as well as those under supervision are met. I would expect those services to maintain the high standards of professionalism in public protection that the public has always seen from the Probation Service.

The Probation Service is, in my view, a vital contributor to public safety and I congratulate the Service on 100 proud years and look forward to the next 100 years.

David Hancock, former Chief Probation Officer, Nottinghamshire

In more recent years the Service has strengthened itself by managing the ambiguity of difficult issues with that same commitment to growth through openness and integrity. Care and control; partnership and contestability; our history and future are full of responses to ambiguity. The capacity to turn an either/or situation into a both/and one requires patience, and often courage. I find that in probation.

I have seen a probation perspective add value in inter-agency settings on so many occasions. Whether at MAPPA, DAT or the Criminal Justice Board, it is probation's capacity to act creatively on the edge of different value systems that counts. Individuals and organisations have varying norms and cultures. In my experience probation staff seem especially attuned to this, and recognise that an idea that may have value for one, can cause offence to another. If a person is invited to look at something from the perspective of another, the ambiguity may be highlighted, and new insights discovered with beneficial results.

Richard Heller, writer

My late partner was a probation officer. Through her and her colleagues I had ten years' education in the role of the probation services. I never saw her at work directly but I often heard her side of long telephone conversations or helped her find the right words for a report. I learnt how much judgment, imagination and sheer energy are demanded from probation officers, as they balance the demands of rehabilitating offenders, protecting the public and serving the interests of justice. I know how they have to struggle to engage with offenders who are sometimes evil but more often damaged and disorganized. Particularly with young offenders, I know that probation officers can make the difference between ruined lives and at least a chance of success. I saw offenders distraught at her death. It grieves me now to see the probation service threatened by shrill and ignorant media and a dogmatic government which believes that big business is invariably superior to public service. I hope that the public probation service survives the next ten years, let alone another century.

Roger Hill, Director of the National Probation Service

The best advocates for the achievements of the service are those whose lives have been changed by their experience: people who have broken the law but worked to repair the damage by servicing their own rehabilitation. We are not naïve or gullible, but there is an idealism, backed by experience, that people can be helped to change from within. It is experience that makes perseverance part of the probation psyche, and something that, as a discipline, will be carried through into the future generations. One hundred years is an important milestone that measures the distance travelled, not the end of the journey.

Baroness Elspeth Howe, former Chair, Equal Opportunities Commission

May I add my warm congratulations to the many you will have received on this very special birthday. During the 26 years I spent as a magistrate – the last twenty of them as one of Inner London's Juvenile Court Chairmen – I developed a healthy respect for the particular skills and expertise Probation Officers brought to our joint work, with the often very difficult as well as troubled youngsters who found themselves before our Juvenile Courts.

And that view was certainly reinforced during my time as a member of the Parole Board (1972-75). Faced with the far from easy decisions as to whether an often dangerous prisoner had reached the stage when release into the community was both safe and beneficial to all concerned, it was the insight of those Probation Officers' detailed reports which so expertly guided us towards the appropriate decision.

I hope the Probation Service will long be able to continue its vital service to the community. However, with many others I remain concerned about how Government plans for the Probation Service are intended to work in the future – particularly whether the present high level of qualification and training required for Probation work will be maintained. If one thing is clear, it is that the current high level of skills has never been more needed than today.

Lord Douglas Hurd, former Home Secretary

For more than twenty years now I have been able to watch the steady progress of the Probation Service. Its work is not always as clearly known or understood as it should be, but I have seen it grow steadily in importance.

It is no exaggeration to say that our society depends in large part on our ability to prevent offending and to deal with offenders in a spirit of understanding rather than despair or vindictiveness. The task of helping the offender without condoning the offence is not easy and is often misunderstood. So these have not been easy years for the Probation Service, quite apart from the constant reorganisation which seems to be the fate of most public bodies. But I have admired the steadfastness with which it has worked and I am sure it will

Lee Jasper, Mayor of London's Director for Equalities and Policing

I want to congratulate the Probation Service on its Centenary and to take this opportunity to commend the invaluable but often unnoticed contribution it makes to society, day in, day out. I have absolutely no doubt that the Probation Service is one of the country's most important public services.

All of us benefit when offenders receive the support and supervision they need to stay away from crime and to rebuild their lives. We must not take the hard work, achievements and commitment to equalities of the Probation Service for granted. It is essential we ensure that the Probation Service receives the support it needs to undertake what is one of the most challenging jobs in modern day Britain

LONDON

Baroness Veronica Linklater, Liberal Democrat

It is extraordinary to think that the Probation Service is 100 years old, pre-dating as it does Beveridge and the post war legislation which gave birth to the Welfare State. Those liberal principles which underpinned the new national framework represented the belief that there should be a safety net for everybody for which Government – and society as a whole – would be responsible. But the Probation Service was there first!

The central tenets of the Service's work were to 'advise, assist and befriend', and how good and appropriate they were then and remain so today. In today's world, the role of enforcement has come to the fore in the process of reorganisation and repeated reorganisation. But I believe that the Service still understands that without the capacity and the space to give advice, guidance and friendship to its clients its essential role would be lost. To be primarily enforcers would be to deny what a probation officer still does which is the tough task of guiding people away from offending, the courts and re-offending and which is achieved through its professionalism and remaining true to its core beliefs.

I salute the Service on its 100th birthday and wish it all that is best today as well as luck for its future. It deserves it.

Veronica Linklater

Elfyn Llwyd MP,
Leader Plaid Cymru

I have always had the highest regard for the Probation Service. Their professionalism and commitment have drastically improved the lives of countless thousands. In turning people away from crime and assisting in making offenders responsible members of society they are worth their weight in gold. Forget NOMS, what we want is a properly resourced Probation Service.

Rod Morgan, Chair, Youth Justice Board

The evidence is that the public understood – more so than other aspects of the justice system – the terms 'Probation Service', 'being on probation' and 'community service'. Moreover for most of the twentieth century the Probation Service believed in itself, which is why it established credibility both at home and internationally. There was need for change in the mission and the manner in which services were delivered. But for various reasons much of the service's self-belief and the public understanding it enjoyed was lost in the run in to and immediately following the new millennium. The service was cast adrift in a sea of structural uncertainty, incoherent management-speak, ideologically-driven poor leadership and political vacillation. It is not too late for the service to regain its poise, and its balls. It still has a vital job to do. What it must not be is dismembered. It must be the coherent lead agency for the execution of criminal court orders. But like the reformed youth justice system it must be wedded to the other mainstream agencies for the delivery of social services and it must be accountable locally.

Lord Phillips of Worth Matravers CJ,
Lord Chief Justice

The supervision of offenders after release from prison or where serving community sentences has become an increasingly vital part of our criminal justice system. For one hundred years we have relied on the dedication of the Probation Service for this critically important work. Society is indebted to them.

Lord David Ramsbotham, former Chief Inspector of Prisons, Cross-Bencher

During the past 100 years the Probation Service has established an enviable record of devoted attention to its role of protecting the public by its supervision of offenders. As it enters its second centenary year it is faced by multifarious challenges, the vast majority are not of its own making. As always the main burden of these will fall on the greatest strength of the Service – its staff. I am constantly amazed by the way in which they continue with their tasks despite being denied too many of the resources that they need them carry it out.

I have two hopes for the Probation Service in its centenary year. First that the public will learn to appreciate the size and scope of the debt that it owes to the men and women of the Service. Second that the government will realise that, if its stated aims are to be satisfied, it must enable those who have to do the various required tasks to do them effectively. It is worth the investment.

Ellie Roy, Chief Executive, Youth Justice Board

Any account of the history of the Probation Service will describe its role in developing constructive alternatives to custody for over a century. This is crucial to understanding and valuing the contribution which the service has made and can continue to make in the future. It also accounts for the fact that representatives from countries across the world continue to visit the UK to learn about the Probation Service, as they seek to develop their own penal systems in a humane and just manner.

Rt Revd Dr Peter Selby, Bishop of Worcester and Bishop to HM Prisons

The importance of the Probation Service cannot be exaggerated. Its history of care for people for whom others do not care too much is so honourable that we must both remember it and conserve it for the present and future. The rehabilitation of those who have offended must be our top priority, and the Probation Service and its members have a hugely important contribution to make to that.

Mark Serwotka, General Secretary, PCS

PCS wishes to congratulate Napo on the occasion of the centenary of the Probation Service. PCS members in the justice system, particularly in the courts and prisons, who work alongside Napo colleagues are reliant on the high quality services and professionalism of probation officers and the probation service in their working lives. For many years PCS has stood shoulder to shoulder with Napo in fighting to preserve the integrity and quality of our justice system and to defend it against the many attempts which have been mounted in order to privatise and profiteer within the justice sector. We also thank Napo members for their solidarity with us in our disputes to preserve services and fight for fair pay for our members. We are pledged, with you, to continue the fight to maintain a high quality professional probation service for the benefit of society as a whole.

Baroness Vivien Stern, former Director of NACRO, Cross-Bencher

The Probation Service of England and Wales sprang from a desire to rescue people from the cruelties of early 20th century imprisonment and help them back into society. Over the years it grew into a model for the rest of the world and was copied by many. It showed how important it is that a penal system should be balanced between retribution and social reintegration. It showed the importance of putting work with those who have broken the law within a strong ethical framework. Those who have power over others and no value base can do terrible things to their fellow human beings. We can only hope that these strengths survive the pressures of the modern world.

Lord Woolf of Barns, former Lord Chief Justice

I am delighted to be able to congratulate the Probation Service on its centenary. Ever since I started practising, approaching fifty year's ago, I have been an admirer of the service. I feel that it is capable of making a huge contribution and my only sadness is that during most of the period to which I have referred, the Service has not been resourced in the way it should be. If it had been, I am sure that our prisons would be operating more effectively and the public would be better protected than they are now.

Brian Strutton, National Officer, GMB

So often unfairly criticised, probation staff provide a highly professional service in the most testing circumstances. Those staff should be trusted to continue to make the Probation Service the vital component in the justice system that it is.

Heather Wakefield, National Secretary, UNISON

'UNISON congratulates the Probation Service on its Centenary. The job that the Service does is fundamental to any civilised society. Protecting the public and helping offenders to change their lives is immeasurably important. The fight for a locally provided, fully accountable and publicly run Probation Service has never been more important.'

UNISON
the public service union

Thanks are due to all those who contributed to this book and all those many probation staff and Napo members who have contributed over the years to make the Probation Service in England and Wales the successful service that it is.

Napo's history is integrally entwined with the history of the Probation Service and the production of this book is indicative of Napo's commitment to celebrate the achievements of the Service over the past century. Celebrating the history of the Service is also useful reminder of what we are currently campaigning to save, given the current threats to its future.

The oral histories covered in this book demonstrate clearly that the success of the Probation Service over the past century is a success based on the passion, the values, the professionalism and the vocation which staff members bring to their work. Probation structures have changed over the decades, just as Napo itself has changed, a change well indicated by the pictures on the front cover.

Throughout the past 100 years and into the next 100 years, probation structures will continue to change, but the central core of the Probation Service will always be based on a commitment to 'Changing Lives.'

Judy McKnight
Napo General Secretary